URBAN
MINISTRY
FROM START TO FINISH

HOW TO DEVELOP AND MAINTAIN A BALANCED
AND LIFE-CHANGING URBAN YOUTH MINISTRY

D1737081

JEFFREY WALLACE

Urban Ministry from Start to Finish
How to Develop and Maintain a Balanced and Life-Changing Urban Youth Ministry

simplyyouthministry.com
group.com

Credits
Author: Jeffrey Wallace
Executive Developer: Nadim Najm
Chief Creative Officer: Joani Schultz
Editors: Christopher Brooks and Rob Cunningham
Cover Art Director: Veronica Lucas
Designer: Veronica Lucas
Production Manager: DeAnne Lear

ISBN 978-0-7644-6769-1

10 9 8 7 6 5 4 3 2 1   20 19 18 17 16 15 14 13 12 11

Printed in the United States of America.

DEDICATION

This book is dedicated to all of the unsung heroes in the trenches of urban youth ministry. Your voice is being heard, your heart is being felt, and your labor is much appreciated. You all inspire me more than you will ever know and I'm your biggest fan! Let's finish strong! God bless you!

—Jeffrey

CONTENTS

CONTENTS

CONTENTS

LETTER FROM ANTHONY FLYNN

Faithful Servant:

We live in a world where the dynamics of culture are changing at an exponential rate. The phenomenon of globalization is sweeping through the streets of historically untapped cities and communities throughout the United States as well as most other cities and communities all over the planet. One of the strongest effects of such evolution is the impact on the local church. Our youth are faced with a multiplicity of dilemmas, including but not limited to the negative effects of social networking, economic uncertainty, confused sexuality, educational disparities, division in government, and much more. In the midst of the crises that continue to arise and force their place into culture, the next generation of youth are grossly perplexed about where to turn.

Building and sustaining a relevant, practical, and magnetizing urban youth ministry is certainly one of the best ways to respond! With the expansion of current issues as well as the evolution of many others in their developmental stages, there has never been a more challenging and demanding time for the universal church to take a stand and intervene on behalf of the last, the lost, and the least of this emerging urban generation. No matter where you are in ministry, no matter how large or how small your budget, team, building, or community is, you have the authority to respond.

In *Urban Ministry From Start to Finish*, Jeff Wallace has leveraged his years of practical, hands-on experience in developing both people and systems to provide you with the tools you will need to create an irresistible youth ministry for this generation. Upon thoroughly examining this resource and then taking the next steps to apply what you have learned, you can count on seeing a drastic shift in the right direction for your leaders, your students, and your ministry context. On your mark, get set, GO and change the world...one student at a time!

Anthony M. Flynn
Urban Youth Workers Institute
Chief Operating Officer
uywi.org

LETTER FROM JEFFREY WALLACE

Hello friends,

After more than 10 years in local ministry, I have found that one of the biggest issues urban youth leaders face is discovering how to build and maintain a healthy and sustainable youth ministry. Perhaps you're wondering, "What is the first thing I need to do when I'm beginning to establish a youth ministry in an urban community or inner city?" This is a great question! Maybe you feel you don't have the ability or the talent to reach this generation that loves the hip-hop culture and operates through all types of social media like Twitter® and Facebook®. Maybe you know you have a call to minister to this group of students, but you lack the practical, relevant, and necessary tools and resources.

If any of these obstacles describe you, then you have picked up the right resource! *Urban Ministry From Start to Finish* will equip you with the necessary tools for building an authentic and sustainable urban ministry, along with motivation and inspiration to help you take your ministry and its leaders to the next level of effectiveness. As a leader, two important keys to your ministry are assembling the right ministry model to fit the culture of your youth group and empowering the right leaders to fulfill the mission and to do the work of the ministry. This resource is a catalytic tool to help you do just that! This manual is not "THE" way—it's "A" way. You're still going to have to add your own personal flavor to the resources provided in order to connect with the students in your area.

As you may have experienced, many potential leaders are hesitant to volunteer and serve. You have the opportunity to show them that youth ministry is worth every ounce of their time, effort, and investment. That's why it's so important that you be equipped with ideas and information and strategies. No matter what your current level of leadership is, *Urban Ministry From Start to Finish* will give you the tools you need and the "how to's" for building, cultivating, and sustaining a healthy, vibrant ministry and ministry team. Your ministry will grow healthier as you and the people around you grow healthier.

As you begin the journey toward a new level of leadership and focus in ministry, I pray that you will receive all of the blessings that God has for you and your ministry.

We're all on the same team!

Jeff Wallace

THE URBAN MISCONCEPTION

People have so many misconceptions about what urban youth ministry really is or which teenagers it really relates to. So what is urban youth ministry, *really*? Is it a "black thing" only found in "black church" youth ministry or is it an approach to ministry that speaks to all ethnic and racial groups? Is it about location or culture? Is it youth ministry that only speaks to inner-city and metropolitan students?

Is it youth ministry that ministers to two-parent households with affluent upper- and middle-class working families—you know, like the Cosbys? Is it an in-your-face youth ministry that speaks to students who've been raped, molested, or abused; to students who cut themselves or think about suicide; to gang bangers, dropouts, dope boys and weed heads, kids in the hood, and baby mommas and baby daddies? Is it a youth ministry with students who love graffiti, hip hop, and R&B and are comfortable using slang or urban jargons like *pimpin*, *crunk*, *what it do*, *holla at me*, and *swagged out*?

Those of us who have worked in urban ministry for any length of time would answer those questions by saying, "YES!" Urban youth ministry is all of those things and so much more. The needs for urban students are as diverse as the cultures, ethnic groups, and personalities of those who make up the urban youth ministry audience.

Because of the diversity of the urban experience, I don't believe there is only one set "cookie cutter" way or magical approach to developing a fundamentally sound, organized urban youth ministry. I do believe, however, that a few essential ingredients will add structure, excitement, and flavor to your ministry and will keep your students coming back week after week.

As a youth pastor in an urban church for more than 10 years, I haven't had the big budget or the fancy facilities. I've learned how to do a lot with very little, and I've learned how to adjust my program or activity according to the current trend or tragedy. In urban ministry, whether you're full time, part time, or bi-vocational, if you're going to be successful, then you have to learn quickly how to be creative and flexible! You can't be married to traditions and church politics, and you definitely can't be OK with "business as usual." If you are reluctant to change, then you're resisting being relevant.

Young Life founder Jim Rayburn once said, "It is a sin to bore kids with the Bible." In urban settings, it is important to keep the Word of God and the flow of your service or program as hot and fresh as ever. Urban students are highly creative and artsy, and if you want to engage them and keep them coming back with their friends, you have to be committed to "flippin' the script" on them as much as possible. If they can predict what you're going to do or say before you do it, you've just lost them, and now you're labeled "lame" or "mad boring" and you've lost the necessary momentum needed to build a successful program.

When I started in youth ministry, I decided that as long as it didn't compromise the message of Jesus Christ, I would do whatever it took to reach students. How far are you willing to reach within yourself to reach urban students? Remember what Paul told the church in Corinth? *Yes, I try to find common ground with everyone, doing everything I can to save some. I do everything to spread the Good News and share in its blessings (1 Corinthians 9:22b-23).*

Let me give you a little more background before you go any further into this resource. I value the importance of having fun, building relationships, and not taking yourself too seriously. I wish I could say all my students come to church because they love to hear me preach the Word of God and because of their love for God and desire to develop a deep commitment to him! Sorry folks, that just ain't true! It's probably not true for you either. Let's face it. The vast majority of unchurched urban students initially come to youth group for the three F's: food, fun, and fellowship!

At my church in Decatur, Georgia (Peace Baptist Church), I'm very intentional in the way I program. We play a lot of games and loud music, mostly hip hop and urban gospel; we go on *cheap* retreats, camps, and trips; we have lock-ins and all-nighters; and most importantly, we develop close, meaningful friendships with as many students as possible. Our weekly youth services are high energy, very lively, and filled with a lot of variety. We infuse several media and arts elements into our services. We use such elements as dramas and skits, dance and videos, and illustrative messages.

Some people will call that being gimmicky or entertaining. I say, "Yes it is!" The games and the fun are just a part of what we do in our youth ministry. It is not all we do. I've found that most urban students don't care how much I know; they want to know how much I care. Dr. Howard Hendricks said, "You can impress people from a distance, but you can only impact them up close." Once people can trust you, they will break down their defensive walls and be more open to receive the Word of God. Paul told the church of Thessalonica: *We loved you so much that we shared with you not only God's Good News but our own lives, too (1 Thessalonians 2:8).*

Another thing I value is the necessity of getting students involved. You don't need a big marketing budget; all you need is a student who loves the youth group. Students are the best marketing tools, especially in urban settings. It's what I like to call "street cred!" If they are proud of their youth ministry or if they're performing at a Sunday or midweek service, trust me, they're going to want *all* of their friends to know about it and see it.

It has been my experience that many students leave the church because of a lack of opportunity to get involved. Students want to feel valued and significant. Make your youth ministry a warm, loving place where students feel like they belong. The reason why gangs, cults, and clubs are so appealing is because they immediately give teenagers a sense of belonging and involvement.

A notorious gang leader once said, "We will always get the youth because we know how to make them feel important." When we in the church don't make teenagers feel important or get them involved, then we've just contributed to lures and traps of a negative society that teaches lonely teenagers how to be pimps, players, wannabes, and thugs. They must be our first priority.

The most important thing I value is the need to be consistent! In urban settings, if you're not in it for the long haul, then don't get in it at all. Urban youth ministry is a marathon; it's not a sprint. Success doesn't always happen overnight. It happens over time. You may have a lot of students without a father in the home who move frequently and change neighborhoods, friends, and schools. So, if there is *one* thing that should remain consistent, it should be their urban youth group that speaks to their urban issues in their urban language! You can do this because Jeremiah 1:5 says, *"I knew you before I formed you in your mother's womb. Before you were born I set you apart and appointed you as my prophet to the nations."*

If you're living in an urban setting, ministering to urban teenagers, then God has equipped you with all the urban resources you need to be successful! Let's get it!

REAL TALK
GOD'S VIEW OF YOUTH MINISTRY

The Bible talks a lot about principles and truths that we can apply to our youth ministries. Teenagers and children have always been an important part of God's eternal plan. The Israelites were given specific instructions to train their young people in the things of God. Deuteronomy 6:1-9 reveals a two-fold reward for obedience: Things would go well, and the nation would increase mightily.

God chose Abraham as a covenant partner on the basis of his willingness to train his offspring (Genesis 18:19). And God used young people throughout the Old Testament to accomplish his will on the earth. Consider these examples. A young David delivered Israel by killing Goliath (1 Samuel 17). The testimony of Naaman's wife's maid led him to receive his healing (2 Kings 5). As a young boy, Samuel had a visit from the Lord telling him of the judgment that would fall on Eli's house (1 Samuel 3). And the children of Israel were used in spiritual gifts (Isaiah 8:18).

TIP
Preach a sermon series for your students based on these passages from the Old and New testaments. Better yet: Ask your senior pastor if you can preach about this topic on a Sunday morning so your whole congregation recognizes God's concern for teenagers!

Jesus' ministry included a focus on children and teenagers, and many of these moments are recorded in the Gospels. He raised the 12-year-old daughter of Jairus from death (Mark 5:22-43). He cast out demons from two children—a girl and a boy (Matthew 15:21-28; 17:14-18). Jesus taught that God rewards people who display kindness to the "least" of his followers (Matthew 10:42). He taught his disciples to respect children and not to offend them (Matthew 18:1-10). The disciples seemed to have forgotten their lesson from that chapter, so Jesus demonstrated that he was not too important for children by taking them into his arms and blessing them (Matthew 19:13-15). Young people surrounded Jesus with praise in the Temple (Matthew 21:15-16). And Jesus wept over the children of Jerusalem, because he knew that the children of his day would face the destruction their parents brought upon them (Matthew 23:37)—and indeed, the Romans destroyed the city in 70 A.D.

God has ordained two institutions to train young people. The primary institution is the family; parents are instructed to train children thoroughly at home (Proverbs 13:24; 19:18; 22:6; 23:13-14; 29:15, 17; and Ephesians 6:4). For parents, children are an inheritance from the Lord. But God also created and called the church to train people, including children and teenagers (Matthew 28:20).

Throughout the Bible, we read about instructions and promises God has made about young people—and even specific commandments to them. One important instruction to children is to obey their parents (Ephesians 6:1-3). Our children can be filled with peace and safety (Isaiah 54:13). God said he would pour out his Spirit upon our sons and daughters (Joel 2:28; Acts 2:16-17). God also said that he would close the generation gap (Malachi 4:5-6). Parents whose children are not serving God can intercede for them with a promise from God (Jeremiah 31:15-17).

God has set ministries in the body of Christ for service to all Christians (Ephesians 4:11-16). The ministry of Jesus was multifaceted. He was an apostle, prophet, evangelist, pastor, teacher—and so much more! Every local church has adults whose primary ministry is in the youth and children's ministries—we simply need to follow God's direction in finding them. Ministers to teenagers and children are called by God to serve the people placed in their care. The church—both local and global—will never reach its full potential without an effective, sustained ministry to youth and children.

The truth is, repetition is a great way for adults to learn, too. Many of the teaching principles you use with teenagers can apply to adult settings, too.

But it's also important to remember that teenagers are not adults and must be taught accordingly. Although they can learn many things, most are not capable of retaining as much truth at one time as adults are. Students must be taught with creative repetition (Isaiah 28:9-10). If they don't understand the Word of God, it will not profit them (Matthew 13:19). To be effective, youth pastors must learn to identify with the teenagers they teach (1 Corinthians 9:19-23). They are capable of choosing to follow Jesus and experience change, healing, and blessing in almost every way that adults can.

Interestingly, parents' faith is often necessary for youth to receive blessings from God. The Gospels record four times Jesus ministered to specific children; three of these stories featured parental faith. He did a miracle out of compassion for the fourth parent, the widow of Nain. God will honor the faith of teenagers, even when their parents are not followers of Christ.

One of the primary functions of youth ministry is to teach the Word of God in a way that reaches both the hearts and minds of students. Although the absence of youth from adult worship, classes, services, and meetings may be convenient for adults, the purpose of the youth service is not to baby-sit. The teacher's primary purpose is to present the Word of God in such a manner that teenagers will understand it and will be able to apply what they have heard to their everyday lives. The teacher should expect and allow room for the Holy Spirit to move in the midst of teenagers. Youth pastors and volunteer leaders must prepare thoroughly. It's important to have a well-planned schedule that includes worship, drama, video, prayer, a message, and other elements that will engage teenagers. The teacher must be spiritually prepared by spending time praying, fasting, and studying the Word of God.

The teacher must present the Word creatively. Use appropriate personal illustrations. Refer to interesting news events, magazine articles, or other media to reinforce truth. Choose drama sketches that reinforce the message. Use appropriate video clips and skits.

Invitations, altar calls, and times of prayer are opportunities for teenagers to respond to the moving of God's Spirit. Prepare the invitation or opportunity so that it is directly related to the teaching and worship that the students have just experienced. Be clear and concise. Don't apply heavy pressure. Teenagers are sensitive enough without it, and the response is God's job, not ours. Provide frequent opportunities for prayer, healing, salvation, and other experiences that are critical to your context in ministry. Train your adult leaders to be ready to explain to teenagers how to respond to God's move.

TIP
You know the style and personality of your congregation. Don't feel constrained to mimic every aspect of your adult services, but also respect the format and approach used by your senior pastor.

Let music be your helper in creating the right atmosphere for the Word. At the beginning of the service, use lively songs to channel the teenagers' energy. Next, sing slower songs to "gear down" for worship. Be diverse in choosing your music styles; you never know which songs may move the hearts of your students—and leaders.

It's important for your youth program to have an intentional, agreed-upon code of discipline. Find out your senior pastor's stance before you use any method of discipline. Develop a disciplinary plan that you consistently follow. Train all of your leaders in the behavior expectations that you have designed, and make sure they know how to appropriately respond to different scenarios. The youth pastor must maintain an appropriate level of control of the class or service; don't let disruptive teenagers take control in an unhealthy fashion.

REAL TALK
ADOLESCENT DEVELOPMENT

Between the ages of 12 and 18, students will go through a variety of different stages of adolescent development. These stages deal with their physical, emotional, social, intellectual, and spiritual needs and development. If you're going to be an effective youth leader that connects and engages with students, then you will need to study and understand this section before you begin programming for your students.

According to kidsgrowth.com, pre-teens and teenagers develop in three phases:

LEVEL I
Early Adolescence (12-13 years old)

Physical
- Changes are rapid and dramatic
- Stamina is lacking; tiredness and short attention span are common
- Awkward moments are frequent; hands and feet are large in proportion to rest of body
- Begins to show physical signs of sexual maturation; emergence of secondary sexual characteristics
- Girls are usually more mature than boys, entering puberty up to two years earlier
- Most have seemingly superhuman appetites

Emotional
- Begins to develop personal identity and sense of self
- Self-conscious and egocentric, but gaining more confidence
- Enthusiastic
- Dependent on parents, but desire for independence is increasing
- Fluctuates between friendly and moody
- Expresses a positive sense of humor

TIP

Offer this information to your adult leaders. Help them understand how teenagers develop during adolescence. Your older student leaders might also appreciate this knowledge!

Social

- Places great value on same-sex peer acceptance; wants to fit in with crowd
- Looks to attach to a few close friends; often cliquish
- Can be overcritical and have unrealistic expectations
- Begins to be interested in opposite sex; girls develop interests earlier
- Develops crushes and identifies heroes
- Most comfortable in small groups of trusted friends of the same sex

Intellectual

- Wants to see proof; less willing to accept others' beliefs (particularly parents' beliefs)
- Begins to think abstractly, but usually views issues in terms of black-or-white answers; increasingly uses reason and logic
- Enjoys problem solving by looking at alternatives and consequences

Spiritual

- Generally receptive to making a decision about a relationship with Christ
- More able to make genuine commitments
- Develops a more sensitive view of right and wrong
- Usually mirrors parents' spiritual views initially
- Begins to develop personal values
- Responds to needs of others; more aware of social issues

LEVEL II
Middle Adolescence (14-15 years old)

Physical

- Physical changes have slowed for girls; boys may still be changing rapidly

- Advanced development of secondary sexual characteristics
- Develops intense sex drive, particularly males
- Active and energetic
- Tends to experiment with alcohol or drugs

Emotional
- Ability to form personal relationships increases
- Less egocentric; learns how to give sacrificially and receive from others
- Often enjoys arguments
- Feels intense need to separate from parents
- Self-assurance can mask deep-felt insecurities and self-doubts
- Seeks recognition for being good in some activity

Social
- Focus moves from same-sex friendships to opposite-sex friendships; dates in groups
- Stays with established circle of friends
- May join a group with social beliefs or values that differ from parents
- Sometimes rebels against people in authority
- May become very protective of personal possessions

Intellectual
- Becomes capable of more complex and abstract thoughts
- Can ask deep questions
- Often questions illogical arguments
- More analytical and critical about belief systems

Spiritual
- Searches for what the Bible says about what is or isn't OK
- May experience guilt about relationships with or thoughts about opposite sex

- May experience frustration with desire to stop some behavior and the apparent inability to do so (such as struggles with pornography or masturbation)
- Often prays for forgiveness

LEVEL III
Late Adolescence (16-18 years old)

Physical
- Physique is almost fully developed
- Boys have caught up with girls developmentally
- Majority have reached adult height
- Expresses a strong interest in personal health
- May fall victim to eating disorders
- Some are sexually experienced

Emotional
- Feels confidence and security with own identity
- Sometimes sentimental
- Can put others' needs ahead of their own
- Recognizes the need to take more personal responsibility
- Usually friendly toward family

Social
- Desires meaningful relationship with others, including opposite sex
- Dating is frequent
- Personal relationships show increasing commitment; many date one partner exclusively
- Driver's license and graduation will be rites of passage
- Many work part time, resulting in discretionary income

Intellectual

- Becomes increasingly involved with future
- Begins to focus on career choices
- Recognizes that current decisions influence future
- Develops ability to consider many options at once; can process possibilities
- Makes better and more mature decisions
- Might be able to resolve conflicts with judgment

Spiritual

- Shows ability to demonstrate strong commitment to a relationship with Christ
- Moral and spiritual values are tested and challenged
- Understands and cares about how others feel and think
- Becomes interested in life after death
- Asks questions and expresses doubts about their spiritual life, such as assurance of salvation
- Is increasingly able to apply spiritual principles to life, and is able to grasp deeper spiritual concepts

How to add flavor to your M.I.N.I.S.T.R.Y.

When designing your ministry, make sure you add flavor and relevance to your program. You only get one chance to make a first impression, so make it a good one! If you're going to have an authentic **M.I.N.I.S.T.R.Y.**, you need:

Massive Outreach: Think beyond the walls of your own church. Place the Great Commission at the center of your praying, planning, training, and programming.

Involve Students: Believe that youth ministry is more than just adults hanging out with teenagers and their friends. It's important that adults help teenagers take ownership of their faith by providing them with opportunities for doing ministry as they discover their giftings and talents.

Numerical Growth: Believe that God cares about numbers, because there are significant numbers of teenagers in your city who don't have a relationship with Christ. In the book of Acts, early church converts were added daily, and God's heart for expanding his kingdom numerically hasn't changed.

Inspirational Fun: God has created teenagers with a soul and body, not just a spirit! So, provide wholesome social and physical activities they will enjoy. The time your students spend in your youth ministry should be some of the most enjoyable and fun times they experience in their teenage years!

Spiritual Growth: Commit to teaching, discipling, challenging, and maturing teenagers in their faith and in the Word of God—spiritually mobilize them to walk in their purpose and destiny, and help them to experience victory over temptation and difficult circumstances.

Seriously, there are few things as exciting as seeing young people stand up and really own their faith. When you see this happen, it will spur you to serve them with even greater passion!

Training Leaders: Your strength rests in the strength of your ministry leadership team, so recruit, equip, and retain gifted leaders to be models of integrity and voices of hope and truth to this generation.

Relevant Worship: Teach students to take their eyes off of the temporal and carnal things of this world, and to worship our Lord and Savior, Jesus Christ, in spirit and in truth. Worship should reflect the diverse styles and sounds of the music that your teenagers listen to on their iPods or MP3 players—but with God-honoring content!

Youth-Friendly Facilities: God created human beings with a need for a desirable environment. For this reason, present an environment for today's teenagers that reflects their styles, tastes, and sounds—not your own. This will create a sense of belonging for them.

GETTING STARTED
MINISTRY ASSESSMENT

When I started in youth ministry, my pastor sat down with me for a conversation. One of his first questions caught me by surprise: "How will you structure the youth ministry to include some kind of succession plan?" I didn't know how to answer! I remember thinking to myself, "Am I getting fired—just after getting hired?" This particular line of questioning was interesting because I was just starting in this role, but he was asking me questions about how people would run the ministry if I weren't there. So, not knowing how much job security I had, I began to develop a leadership manual that would become the youth ministry resource bible for our church. Habakkuk 2:2 says, *"Write my answer plainly on tablets."* How true that is! People will never follow you if they don't know where you are going.

So, a good first step in developing a healthy urban youth ministry is to assess your current situation and ask yourself and your key leaders—if you have any—a few questions. This assessment will help you determine your strengths, weaknesses, threats, and opportunities for growth. To help you assess and gauge where you are in your ministry development, I've provided a set of questions. Think about the current state of your youth ministry and then circle either **TRUE** or **FALSE** for each question.

- A key leader has been clearly identified and is responsible for the youth ministry. This leader has a written job description.

   TRUE or **FALSE**

- If the key leader of the youth ministry resigned today, a new leader would have a written record of how the ministry operates and flows.

   TRUE or **FALSE**

- Job descriptions of each person in the youth ministry are clearly defined and understood by people involved in the ministry.

  TRUE or **FALSE**

- The church has a written description of the youth ministry, and church leaders are aware of who the key leader is.

  TRUE or **FALSE**

- The youth ministry operates from a set of annual goals and objectives that are reviewed regularly.

  TRUE or **FALSE**

- Leaders involved in the youth ministry have a working knowledge of the annual budget.

  TRUE or **FALSE**

- Leaders involved in the youth ministry have a working knowledge of the policies and procedures—or a copy of the policy manual—required by church leadership.

  TRUE or **FALSE**

- Leaders in the youth ministry have a copy of the master calendar of youth events, activities, and meetings for the current year.

  TRUE or **FALSE**

- The youth ministry has clearly defined marketing, advertising, and promotional plans for the year.

  TRUE or **FALSE**

- The church staff has regular and easy access to a written plan of your facilities and equipment usage for the current year.

   TRUE or **FALSE**

- A formal training course is currently in place for anyone who becomes involved as a leader in the youth ministry.

   TRUE or **FALSE**

TOTAL SCORE:

True _____   False _____

If you have 1 to 3 True responses (9 to 7 False responses), you fall into the "911" phase. You're probably a one-person show, and the ministry probably is built around you. If you fall into this category, use this manual to help you map out a blueprint for your urban ministry. Set aside some time and dream about how you want your youth ministry to function. Get a core group of leaders to go through this manual with you and work out a plan for developing a balanced, healthy, life-changing ministry.

If you have 4 to 8 True responses (6 to 2 False responses), you fall into the "In Too Deep" phase. A lot of ministries fit this category. You're not in the 911 phase, but you do have areas of importance that are lacking and holes that need to be filled. You must not get comfortable being good, when God wants you to be great! Be honest about the areas that need to be improved and then be intentional about addressing those areas.

If you have at least 9 to 10 True responses (and 1 to 0 False responses), you fall into the "VIP" phase. You're doing great! Continue to build on the solid foundation. One word of caution: Even though you're at VIP status today, remain focused on God's plans for your ministry and stay aware of current trends, topics, issues, and social networking opportunities. Even though you have a great system in place, it will be ineffective if the message is irrelevant.

In the development of any organization, vision and mission statements provide a foundation for building a leadership structure. They serve as a blueprint to your program. These statements offer current and future leaders a clear snapshot of your ministry, its direction, and its potential target audiences. In structuring your urban youth ministry, your vision and mission statements are vital.

A **vision statement** is a picture of your ministry in the future. Your vision statement is your inspiration—the framework for your strategic planning. A **mission statement** is a brief description of your ministry's fundamental purpose. Your mission statement answers the question, "Why do we exist?"

The mission statement articulates the ministry's purpose both for those in the ministry and those outside of the ministry. The difference between a mission statement and a vision statement is that a mission statement focuses on the ministry's current state, while a vision statement focuses on the ministry's future.

A vision statement may apply to the entire youth ministry or to a single part of the youth ministry (worship, outreach, discipleship, evangelism, or ministry). Whether for all or part of the ministry, the vision statement answers the question, "Where do we want to go?"

Your goal when creating a vision statement is to articulate your dreams and hopes for your ministry. It reminds you of what God placed in your heart when you first answered the call to ministry and how you are striving to fulfill God's plans in your community.

While a vision statement doesn't tell you how you're going to get there, it does set the direction for your ministry planning. That's why it's important when developing a vision statement to let your imagination go and dare to dream—and why it's important that a vision statement captures your passion. Acts 2:17 says, *"In the last days,"* God says, *"I will pour out my Spirit upon all people. Your*

TIP

Remember, these are a foundation—and foundations are things you build on. Be prepared to come back to your vision and mission statements as time passes. What you write today will probably be different from what you'll write in five years, and that's fine!

sons and daughters will prophesy. Your young men will see visions, and your old men will dream dreams." This is your time to seek God's vision and dream for your ministry!

A good vision statement should be no longer than three to five paragraphs. Some questions to consider:

- What do you want your ministry to look like three years from now?
- What target audience do you believe God wants you to reach?
- What new programs and opportunities will you develop?
- How will you expand your efforts to train new adult leaders and give teenagers opportunities to serve?
- What results are you praying God will deliver?

Don't try to be too deep with this. Simple is usually better than complex.

Tie your vision and mission statements to at least one scriptural reference. Once you've developed your vision and mission statements, make sure that you, your leaders, and your students know them and live them. You may want to display them in your youth room, include them on letterhead, and use them wherever you can create visibility for your ministry. The vision and mission statements will assure you that everyone is reading off the same sheet of music. It's also important that your vision and mission statements complement the overall direction of your congregation.

SAMPLE VISION STATEMENT
(Peace Baptist Church Student Ministry Vision Statement)

We envision the Student Impact of Peace Baptist Church being a spiritual organization designed to liberate and empower students to move from living apart from Christ, to serve Christ with all of their heart and soul, and to share him with others. Student Impact will be a place for students to **BELIEVE** in themselves and the power of

God and his Spirit; to **BELONG** to something positive, inspirational, and life-changing; and to **BECOME** a Spirit-filled beacon of light in a dark and dismal world. It is our desire to expose both the churched and unchurched student to the true gospel of Jesus Christ, to help them experience the unconditional love of God, and to equip them to serve and share Christ with everyone they come in contact with.

The driving force behind Student Impact is not based on programs, personalities, or gimmicks, but the eternal purpose of God. Our objective is to share Christ and our faith without fear, build and establish relationships that will never fade, and offer students a sense of hope and comfort in times when they feel hopeless. Our focus is to target any unchurched student and move them to becoming a core, committed student who has discovered his or her spiritual gifts, is serving in a ministry, and shows an understanding of prayer, the Word of God, outreach and evangelism, and missions.

SAMPLE MISSION STATEMENT
(Peace Baptist Church Student Ministry Mission Statement)

Our mission is to **REACH** lost students for Christ **(EVANGELISM)**, **RECONNECT** Christian students with other believers **(FELLOWSHIP)**, help students **RENEW** their faith in God **(DISCIPLESHIP)**, inspire them to **RECYCLE** the gifts God has given them **(MINISTRY)**, and **RESTORE** their lives by teaching them to honor God **(WORSHIP)**.

OUR MISSION STATEMENT'S EXPLANATION

Evangelism: Our mission is to encourage students to **REACH** out to unchurched students and share their faith without fear. God has commissioned us to *"Go and make disciples" (Matthew 28:19).*

Fellowship: Our mission is to promote within our student ministry a spirit of unity. In doing so, students weekly **RECONNECT** with other Christian students and believers.

Discipleship: Our mission is to inspire students to develop a deeper walk with Christ by teaching them how to daily **RENEW** their faith and study God's Word. God has commissioned us to *"Teach these new disciples to obey"* (Matthew 28:20).

Ministry: Our mission is to teach students to **RECYCLE** their God-given talents and gifts for the advancement of the kingdom of God. God has commissioned us to *"Love your neighbor as yourself"* (Matthew 22:39).

Worship: Our mission is to teach students how to be **RESTORED** by loving and honoring God with all of their heart and soul in both the personal and private times of their lives. The Great Commandment says, *"You must love the Lord your God with all your heart, all your soul, and all your mind"* (Matthew 22:37).

GETTING STARTED
SCRIPTURAL FOUNDATIONS

Building a healthy ministry takes more than personalities, people, or programs; you need to build on a scriptural foundation. This keeps your ministry balanced, purposeful, and connected to God's Spirit and presence. Listed below is how I see God's Word tied to our ministry. It was adapted from Doug Fields' *Purpose-Driven Youth Ministry* model.

At Peace Baptist Church, our student ministry is centered on five biblical principles found in two familiar passages from Jesus Christ:

- **The Great Commandment:** *"'You must love the Lord your God with all your heart, all your soul, and all your mind.' This is the first and greatest commandment. The second is equally important: 'Love your neighbor as yourself'"* (Matthew 22:37-39).

- **The Great Commission:** *"Therefore, go and make disciples of all the nations, baptizing them in the name of the Father and the Son and the Holy Spirit. Teach these new disciples to obey all the commands I have given you. And be sure of this: I am with you always, even to the end of the age"* (Matthew 28:19-20).

1. **The Principle of <u>Worship</u>:** *"You must love the Lord your God with all your heart, all your soul, and all your mind"*

2. **The Principle of <u>Ministry</u>:** *"Love your neighbor as yourself"*

3. **The Principle of <u>Evangelism</u>:** *"Go and make disciples"*

4. **The Principle of <u>Fellowship</u>:** *"Baptizing them..."*

5. **The Principle of <u>Discipleship</u>:** *"Teaching these new disciples to obey..."*

TIP

Get your adult and student leaders involved by asking them to search through the Bible for verses or passages that can help form a solid foundation for your youth ministry.

Additional student ministry scriptural foundations:

- *We loved you so much that we shared with you not only God's Good News but our own lives, too (1 Thessalonians 2:8).*

- *Don't let anyone think less of you because you are young. Be an example to all believers in what you say, in the way you live, in your love, your faith, and your purity (1 Timothy 4:12).*

- *But you are not like that, for you are a chosen people. You are royal priests, a holy nation, God's very own possession. As a result, you can show others the goodness of God, for he called you out of the darkness into his wonderful light (1 Peter 2:9).*

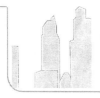

GETTING STARTED
CHARACTER COVENANTS

What do you stand for? How do you define your ministry and leadership DNA? As a ministry leader, what are your absolute, non-negotiable standards? In other words, when you have leaders who are part of your urban youth ministry, what do you expect of them? What are your urban youth ministry's "Core Values" and "Character Covenants"? Here's a list of some values and covenants we use at Peace Baptist Church that act as a base of our urban youth ministry.

AS LEADERS IN THIS STUDENT MINISTRY WE WILL VALUE...

1. **PRAYER:** We value **PRAYER** because it changes things, confirms our vision, cleanses our hearts, and increases our closeness with God.

2. **WORSHIP:** We value **WORSHIP** because it exalts Jesus and edifies individual Christians and the whole body of Christ.

3. **STEWARDSHIP:** We value **STEWARDSHIP** because every Christian should be committed to a life of biblical stewardship, which involves the use of time, talent, and tithe.

4. **GOD'S WORD:** We value **GOD'S WORD** because it equips, encourages, empowers, and inspires us.

5. **EVANGELISM:** We value **EVANGELISM** because Christians should be the salt of the earth and light to people who don't know Jesus, and we should have an effective witness of Christ's love, forgiveness, and reconciliation.

6. **DISCIPLESHIP:** We value **DISCIPLESHIP** because it is our way of further developing and training Christians for continuous work for God's kingdom.

TIP

Do a little research in the Bible about the power of covenants. They're more than just simple commitments. They're life-changing and life-directing opportunities.

TIP

Take these ideas and use them in your own youth ministry. Teach these covenants to your students and your leaders. Adapt them to your own setting. Live them out with your ministry!

7. **UNITY:** We value **UNITY** because it strengthens our witness, fellowship, and ability to endure trials, tribulations, and troubles.

8. **COMMITMENT:** We value **COMMITMENT** because it exemplifies belief and loyalty in the vision and mission of our church as a whole.

9. **FELLOWSHIP:** We value **FELLOWSHIP** because it promotes unity and community within the body of Christ.

10. **EXCELLENCE:** We value **EXCELLENCE** because God is excellent and he is worthy of our very best in all we do, what we say, and how we live.

In the development of your ministry, it is essential that your leaders model the highest level of servant leadership to both God and to the students. For this to be true, each leader should be committed to some core covenant values of your ministry or organization. At Peace Baptist Church, members of the Youth Development Department leadership team have all committed to the following covenants:

1. **Christ-likeness:** We resolve to live as Christ would have us live. We will endeavor to hate what is evil, cling to what is good, and to live as those who are accountable to God first. *So we are Christ's ambassadors; God is making his appeal through us. We speak for Christ when we plead, "Come back to God!" (2 Corinthians 5:20).*

2. **Loyalty:** We resolve to be loyal to one another. We will speak well of each other, stick together in tough times, and believe the best of each other as we serve God and others.

3. **Confidentiality:** We resolve to maintain confidentiality in our interactions with the youth, young adults, and one

TIP

Your leadership team will benefit from understanding and committing to these covenants at the start—and make sure new leaders know them before joining the team.

another. We will make a conscious effort to model a professional code of ministerial ethics regarding honesty in self-disclosure.

4. **Growth:** We resolve to continue to grow in the grace and knowledge of Jesus Christ through regular participation in private and corporate prayer, worship, Sunday Impact classes, and Wednesday Night Live discipleship classes.

5. **Training:** We resolve to take part in ongoing education and training activities, conferences, workshops, and seminars. We will continually strive to sharpen our spiritual gifts in order to improve our leadership effectiveness and influence.

6. **Safe Environment:** We resolve to provide our children and teenagers with the safest environment possible—an environment that protects them from pedophiles, rapists, molesters, pornography, drugs, alcohol, inappropriate relationships, and other harmful or immoral influences. In doing so, *all* Youth Development leaders *must* have a criminal background check done in order to work in the Youth Development Department.

7. **Communication:** We resolve to communicate clearly with one another. We will do our best to maintain clear lines of communication and to coordinate all activities.

8. **Conflict:** We resolve to handle conflicts in a Christ-like manner. We will avoid being overly sensitive or defensive and will deal with conflicts quickly and respectfully.

9. **Creativity:** We resolve to be creative in our attempts to provide programs, ministries, and activities that are relevant, life-changing, and current with the youth culture. We must not think out of the box—we must think beyond the box.

TIP
Here's a great principle: Communicate, communicate, communicate. You really can't overcommunicate when it comes to leadership!

10. Hardship: We resolve to endure hardship as we work together for the cause of Christ. We will work together to encourage one another and lift one another up during times of personal and corporate difficulty.

THE PEOPLE
BUILDING AND RETAINING A GREAT TEAM

When building a team, how do you select quality first-round draft picks?

As you start recruiting the right leaders for your ministry, determine what type of people you believe will be a good fit. Who will have an impact in the lives of your church's teenagers? Who is effective at reaching out to kids outside of the church walls? What type of person will humbly become a tool in God's hands as the team carves out the work that God has put before you? As you think about what type of people you want to have on your team, here are some characteristics and traits to look for in your recruiting process:

1. A desire to serve others

You don't want people who just plan to come and sit around. You don't want people who come to wear a leader shirt and badge. You want people who have a desire and a passion to serve! You want people who have the attitude and mindset of "I'm going to do whatever it takes!"

People with a servant's heart are only satisfied when they please God with their talents and gifts. These people will get behind the vision for the youth ministry because by serving the vision, they ultimately are serving God. Whether it's driving a bus or cleaning a toilet, a person who is willing to serve will have the right motives and is less likely to burn out.

2. A determination to learn

"God blesses those who hunger and thirst for justice, for they will be satisfied" (Matthew 5:6).

You want to recruit and retain leaders who are hungry to serve *and* to learn. Leaders who are hungry to learn will always seek to improve the ministry and will contribute to the results you desire. If your team members are not growing, your ministry will most likely struggle to grow. The difference between success and failure is not strength or knowledge—it is hunger. If your team members possess a strong hunger to learn, they will cultivate an environment of excellence and growth.

Jesus demonstrated servant leadership, he challenged his disciples to pursue that lifestyle, and he challenges us today to pursue it, too.

3. A dedicated heart for teenagers

Did you know that there are people working in youth ministry who don't have a heart for students? I once heard about a frustrated youth pastor who said, "I love youth ministry, but it's the teenagers that I can't stand." Seriously?

If you are going to successfully make an impact on the lives of teenagers, you need leaders who genuinely care for them and are focused on ministering to them and meeting their needs. Teenagers can easily recognize people who don't really care about them. This is the "keep it real" generation. They know a fake person when they see one. Your ministry will be damaged if students believe that a member of your team is "a fake."

Taking time to evaluate potential leaders and even remove current leaders who do not have a real passion for teenagers can be the difference between exploding into new growth instead of spiraling into a rapid downfall. People who are doing ministry only because someone asked them to often lack a heart and passion for teenagers.

SOURCE: Lee Wilson Ministries www.umr-21.com

At this point, I hope you're fired up and ready to go, but there is still more to consider if you want to have a successful recruitment process. Your success is determined by people showing up and getting involved because they know God has called them to this ministry. It's important to establish "buy-in" from your team. Here are four principles to live by when recruiting new leaders for your ministry.

1. Don't judge a book by its cover

Don't disqualify people by what you can see on the outside. Believe it or not, there is gold sitting undiscovered in the pews of your church. Don't stereotype anyone. Get to know prospective leaders, and then come to some conclusions. Your church right now has people who are anointed, gifted, and passionate about reaching students. There are women and men in your congregation who may not appear as though they fit your team, but there's a place that has been established specifically for them when God calls them. Ask God to show you who should be a part of your ministry. Pray fervently for God's provision in the area of youth leaders. Have your students and their parents pray with you. When new leaders do step up, they will immediately be seen as answered prayer! How great would that feel as a new leader?

TIP
Effective leadership is rooted in healthy relationship. The more you get to know people before they join your team, the stronger bond you'll have once they're on board.

2. Develop a recruitment plan because if you fail to plan, you plan to fail

Always plan how you're going to add new leaders to your team. Develop leadership workshops that you schedule separately from your regular youth meetings. These workshops can be held on a Saturday morning, Sunday night, or whatever time works best for you and your team. Use this meeting as a platform to recruit new workers and to get people to share their testimonies about serving in the youth ministry. Be strategic; call on leaders who are excited about working in the ministry. Talk about the vision of your ministry and the things you want to accomplish. Be sure to have applications available, and inform potential leaders how to get involved.

Be excited about your ministry! In all truth, you are helping people grow spiritually by providing a structured opportunity for them to serve in the church. Your job is to simply encourage them to get involved and create an easy, accessible, effective process for them to do it.

3. **Develop a plan for training your leaders**
This plan will equip your leaders and help hold them accountable as they serve in your ministry. Don't just let people come and get involved right away. Give them time—at least a month—to learn about the ministry, see what they are signing up for, and pray for God's leading. If they have not gone through a new members' class at your church, encourage or require them to do so. They will catch the overall vision of the congregation and have a better understanding of how the youth ministry fits into the big picture. Have a face-to-face conversation with them after a month to answer any questions. Interview them before they actually join the team. They need to "see and feel" what the ministry is about before they commit to it. This is important to the goal of retaining leaders and should be on your mind even as you recruit them.

4. **Create recruitment brochures and other promotional materials**
Brochures, video clips, business cards, and other ministry-specific materials are powerful tools that can cause potential leaders to take notice of your ministry. Successful companies put effort into their logos, handouts, brochures, and fliers to make sure that their products are seen and remembered. Put together a recruitment tool that talks about the youth ministry. It could be a flier, calendar, brochure, or a DVD. Make it available in the foyer of your church or some other prominent location. If you can't create a flier, ask your pastor if you can use your church bulletin, church calendar, or the church newsletter to recruit for the youth ministry or talk about an upcoming youth event. Finally, ask your pastor to help you recruit new leaders. Ask your pastor to talk about your ministry's successes and its opportunities from the

TIP
If you're not gifted in this area, turn to adults or students who are! Find creative, talented people who can make your team stronger. Their efforts will bring in more leaders, which will continue the process of strengthening the team.

pulpit on a Sunday morning, and to consider adding it to the announcements. There's something about hearing it from the pastor that causes people to get involved.

Here are some ways you can recruit and assess potential leaders:
- Creating a formal application process
- Explaining the opportunity in church membership classes
- Offering interviews with the youth pastor
- Conducting personality profiles and criminal background checks
- Communicating the need for youth leaders in bulletins, announcements, newsletters, e-mails, and other church publications
- Screening people and having them tell their story of how they began following Jesus and how their personal relationship with Jesus Christ impacts their desire to serve
- Helping prospective youth leaders clarify their call and desire to work with students, and explaining how God's Word guides your expectations of a youth leader

Here are just a few examples of the many different roles leaders can play in your youth ministry:
- Assisting with office tasks
- Teaching Sunday classes
- Coordinating events
- Mentoring teenagers
- Creating promotional and marketing material
- Assisting student musicians, actors, and artists
- Leading small groups
- Coaching other small group leaders
- Providing resources for youth ministry events
- Training teenagers on media, soundboard, or other technical equipment
- Decorating and setting up for special events
- Driving students to and from activities
- Praying with students during youth services

Pause right now and identify at least five opportunities to serve in your church that are *not* on this list. You know you've got 'em!

Some people might be
the wrong fit for your
team *but* they might
be a perfect fit for
another team in your
congregation. These
cases of "wrong fit"
have nothing to do with
personality or problems;
they're just examples of
how God has wired each
person uniquely for
specific roles in serving
the body of Christ.

How do you know which players are *not* right for your team?
Now that you know who you *are* looking for, think about some of the
people who might *not* be a good fit for your team. Here are some
characteristics you probably don't want to see in potential leaders:

- People looking for specific titles
- People looking for prestige or power
- People looking for money or promotion
- People looking for a place to make new "friends" in the
  youth group
- People who are unsupportive of the vision or of church
  leadership

If you avoid people with these characteristics when choosing your
team, you're more likely to avoid unnecessary strife and division
within your ministry. You will also avoid the mess that is created
when a youth leader has to be removed from a role of influence
with students.

You also might want to avoid prospects with these personality traits:

- **"Control freaks."** They will want control—over everything.
- **"Rebels."** They will not listen and follow the chain of
  command, and they will be difficult to correct, guide, or
  mold.
- **"Needy people."** They want to get involved to meet *their*
  needs more than the needs of the students and families in
  the church.
- **"Know-it-alls."** They won't respect your opinion or other
  leaders' opinions. They already have it all figured out!
- **"Wounded soldiers."** They need pastoral care and/or
  professional help. Hurt people hurt other people.

And when thinking about ministry through the lens of heart and
passion, these are people to be cautious of adding to your team:

- Those who want to serve because they're looking for a
  stepping stone to the next level

- Those who stereotype, judge, and generally dislike teenagers
- Those who are just looking to any ministry to serve in; if they are not clear on how they truly feel about teenagers, they may do more harm than good

It's also important to think about the things you should avoid saying when recruiting potential youth leaders. You know the old cliché: You never get a second chance to make a first impression. When your potential youth leaders walk away from an initial conversation with you, they should be inspired, excited, and have a clear and accurate understanding of how they might connect with your ministry. Here are some examples of things you might *not* want to say.

1. **"I know you're really busy, but can you..."**
   We all have busy schedules, and we all have the same 24 hours in each day. There are always a lot of things that we have to do—but we also have the choice on how we use the time God has given us. Don't apologize for asking people to commit to serving in the ministry. This commitment is going to require time. Your volunteers are going to have to prioritize and make a commitment. When your leaders invest time in serving God and his people, they are helping build the kingdom of God—and they are building a solid foundation for their own future. God will give your leaders grace and margin in their lives to do whatever is needed to fulfill his plan. Remember, you want leaders who are willing to sacrifice a portion of their time for God's work.

2. **"Please help us! We desperately need you! You won't have to do much!"**
   Think about the campaign that the U.S. Army used for two decades. The Army didn't recruit by saying, "Can you come and just do a little something?" or "We just need somebody to maybe go over to another country and protect our nation" or "We just need you to kinda protect our country." No! They said, "Be all that you can be!" The church can and should take a cue from the Army!

TIP
But be cautious about adopting one of the Army's other former slogans: "An Army of One." Ministry is about working as a team toward a common goal!

Go with boldness, expecting and encouraging potential leaders to give God their best. God does not need people to serve him partially, without a spirit of excellence and a determination to do great things. God expects the best from all of us, so don't let the people on your team get stuck in mediocrity. Of course, part of your role is to reassure people that you will walk with them, pray with them, equip them, and serve them—but they must be fully in. Our teenagers deserve "all that we can be!"

This doesn't mean people have to quit their jobs to serve God. Absolutely not! And some leadership roles will require a bigger or smaller time commitment than other roles will. But you have the opportunity to motivate leaders to do their best with the skills, gifts, and life experiences that they bring to ministry. Leaders who are willing to do their best, no matter the task, can be agents of growth and change. They will feel fulfilled, and students will love and respect them!

3. **"I'm really desperate for some help. Could you please come join us?"**
When Jesus went to the disciples, he told them that if they followed, he would teach them how to fish for people—they would make a difference. He displayed excitement about the opportunity. He was bold about it. His disciples didn't know where they were really going, but they were following him. They dropped everything and followed the leader.

You don't want to beg people to join your ministry. This signals desperation, and no one wants to board a sinking ship. Desperation leads to a sense of defeat, and defeat leads to a lack of motivation and hope. Begging for involvement becomes a self-fulfilling prophecy for failure.

As you go, go with excitement! People are attracted to confidence and optimism. Advance confidently toward your God-given dreams with optimism about the future of your ministry, and you will attract a passionate, God-focused team.

A PLUG-IN EVENT FOR POTENTIAL LEADERS

Most good things don't just happen; they must be planned! Here are some suggestions on a successful recruitment event that can help get potential leaders officially "plugged in."

1. Advertise your meeting
- Use e-blast messages, fliers, Facebook® announcements, and phone tree
- Include location, date, and start/end times
- Enlist current leaders to invite potential leaders that they may know
- Contact anyone who recently has expressed an interest in getting involved

2. Write out an agenda for your recruitment meeting
- Determine when the meeting will begin and end, and where it will be held
- Create an agenda showing how the meeting will flow
- Determine how the room (tables, chairs, and podium) should be set up

3. Organize all your information before the meeting
- Provide agendas for everyone responsible for the meeting
- Have plenty of applications on hand, and assign a current leader to collect them
- Provide your ministry guidelines
- Provide background check forms
- Provide department descriptions explaining what leadership and service opportunities are available
- Prepare note sheets

4. Communicate with your current leaders
- Discuss the vision and goals for the meeting
- Present their roles for the meeting

TIP

If you typically bring on one or two leaders at a time, this event may be larger than what you need. But you can still adapt the principles of informing prospective leaders, connecting them with current leaders, letting them see how your youth ministry operates, and making yourself available to answer questions. Most of all, make sure people know how to get from interest to involvement.

- Clarify what things you need and when you will need them
- Distribute agendas for the meeting

5. From the beginning, establish the DNA of your leadership
- Personally greet as many people as possible
- Provide refreshments as a form of hospitality
- Welcome everyone and open with prayer (opportunity for students to be involved)
- Organize an icebreaker game or activity to loosen everyone up (opportunity for students to be involved)
- Have a short praise and worship set (opportunity for students to be involved)
- Keep your message brief and keep the tone conversational
- Share the mission of the youth ministry and the rewards of being part of the team
- Share the future of the youth ministry and where you see opportunity
- Invite people to become a part, highlighting specific areas of need
- Announce upcoming events and any other pertinent information (opportunity for students to be involved)
- If possible, use PowerPoint, music, and video clips to enhance your presentation
- Be available to answer any questions
- Use key leaders as much as possible
- Make sure the "next step" is clear so potential leaders can continue through the process

6. Keep your pastor in the loop
- Send an agenda and meeting minutes of the night to your pastor or director

TIP
Don't keep your pastor in the dark. Ever. You're asking for troubles down the road if you do that!

THE PEOPLE
POLICIES AND PROCEDURES

Developing and implementing policies and procedures will contribute to the growth, development, and sustainability of your youth ministry. As the point person of your church's youth ministry, it is essential that you put together clear policies and procedures for your team to follow. Your church may have existing policies that you do not need to re-create, so make sure you review what your church has developed before you begin putting together your youth ministry policies. Also, ask your peers and friends in youth ministry if you can get copies of what they have developed. Finally, when choosing and/or writing policies and procedures, keep them as simple as possible. Don't try to be deep; just make sure that they are clear and realistic.

Here are examples of a Student Leader Expectations form and an Adult Leader Expectations form:

STUDENT LEADER EXPECTATIONS

This is an opportunity for you as a student to participate in and be responsible for one or more parts of this event or program. While serving in any of the ministry's activities, you will be expected to follow certain guidelines and rules. These guidelines are for your own good, as well as for the overall good of the student ministry. By signing this list of expectations, you are committing to live up to each standard, and you are committing to be held accountable for living a life that is holy and acceptable to Christ. If any leader finds you not living up to any of these expectations, you will be asked and expected to correct the problem. If the problem continues, then you will be sent home at your parent(s)' expense (if necessary), and if it continues thereafter, you will need to be accompanied by your parent(s)' during all student activities in which you are involved.

I, _____, agree to the following:

TIP
Some prospective leaders may question the need for a commitment or covenant. Remind them that it isn't a sign of doubt or distrust—it's a way of raising the bar for everyone on the team, in your youth ministry, and in your congregation.

- I will not swear or use any inappropriate language.
- I will not use any drugs, tobacco, alcohol, or other inappropriate substances.
- I will only be able to use CD players and iPods at certain times, regulated by leaders. My musical choices will honor God. Leaders have the right to confiscate devices containing any inappropriate music and return them whenever they feel necessary.
- I will only wear appropriate clothing with logos and symbols that are not offensive or negative in meaning. I will not wear pants that sag (guys), and I will not wear tight-fitted clothing or clothing that reveals my belly button, cleavage, or lower back (girls).
- I will not make fun of anyone or make anyone feel less than what God says they are. My words will build up, edify, encourage, and inspire others, not tear them down.
- I will be where I am supposed to be at all times, and I will be on time for everything to the best of my ability.
- I will not partake in any inappropriate public or private affection, sexual activities, or any other physical activities that are contrary to God's Word.
- I will respect others, all leaders, and adults at all times.
- I will not bring, purchase, or view any questionable books, magazines, or websites.
- I will not complain. I understand that all decisions will be made for the good of the group, not an individual.
- I will have a great attitude toward the activities, trips, retreats, and other events.
- I will always work toward having fun, living life to the fullest, and practicing safety.

I agree to live up to these expectations on all church activities.

Student Signature: _____

Date: _____

I understand that my student is responsible for holding to these expectations, and I have reviewed and understand the consequences if he or she does not.

Parent Signature: _____

Date: _____

ADULT LEADER EXPECTATIONS

Thank you so much for your decision to invest in the lives of our students. Your task is not an easy one, but with God's help, together we can build relationships that will last a lifetime with our students, as they develop into Christian adults and leaders. We want this to be an encouraging opportunity for both you and the students; this is why we have created this list of leadership expectations.

I, _____ commit to the following expectations:

- I have given my whole life to Christ.
- Through my talk and my life, I will conduct myself in a manner that represents Jesus Christ.
- I am pursuing and will continue to pursue personal growth in my walk with Christ in this local church body.
- I understand the importance of discipleship and my role as a leader in this ministry.
- I will live a pure, holy, and acceptable life before God and before all whom I encounter. This means that I will not participate in or practice infidelity, pornography, or other compromising lifestyle behaviors that may destroy my witness.
- I will not date, flirt, go out with, or have sexual relationships or any other inappropriate relationships with ANY of the students within the student ministry.

- I will not dress inappropriately in my daily life or at student ministry functions.
- I understand the importance of men ministering to guys and women ministering to girls.
- I will not smoke, drink, or use any inappropriate or illegal substances.
- I will not place myself in situations and circumstances that will discredit my witness and ministry to others.
- I will commit to be at leadership meetings, retreats, and trainings.
- I will commit to communicating any times I am unable to be at any meetings, classes, or trainings.
- It is my responsibility to be where I say I'm going to be and do what I say I'm going to do.

I understand that no one is perfect, except Christ, but I also understand that ministry rises and falls on leadership. And because of that fact, I commit to giving my very best all the time, coming short some of the time, and giving excuses none of the time!

Dear brothers and sisters, not many of you should become teachers in the church, for we who teach will be judged more strictly (James 3:1).

Signature: _____

Date: _____

Once you have your leaders, effectively train them. A clear and effective training program for leaders will promote balance and health within your team. You can never go wrong with constant and consistent training of your leadership team.

Curriculum used to train leaders

Below are some options for training your youth leaders:

- Create fellowship gatherings and informal coffee times, meals, and gatherings
- Organize structured weekly, monthly, or quarterly meetings
- Provide regularly scheduled workshops, seminars, and prayer times
- Buy them books to learn from on their own time (such as *Purpose-Driven Youth Ministry* by Doug Fields)
- Participate in leadership retreats using a resource like John Maxwell's *Leadership Development Sessions*
- Encourage Bible studies for leaders
- Use spiritual gifts workshops for discovering the right place and way to minister
- Have leaders attend relevant workshops, conventions, and retreats

Training and event calendar

Consider offering the following opportunities for your leaders:

- Weekly Bible study with senior pastor, along with adult worship
- Monthly youth staff meetings
- Quarterly outings for adult leaders (fun and fellowship)
- Monthly leadership training for student leaders
- Quarterly outings for student leaders

TIP
Ultimately, your goal is to create and grow a healthy urban youth ministry. Healthy leaders contribute to healthy ministries.

Evaluations

You can evaluate your youth leaders' growth in ministry and their personal and spiritual growth in the following ways:

- Talk with them about the things they are learning and experiencing, and what God is saying to them through ministry involvement
- Solicit feedback from your senior pastor, parents, and students
- Solicit feedback from other leaders, both within and outside of the youth ministry
- Provide a formal evaluation from the youth pastor

Encouragement

Here are some ways you can encourage your leaders:

- Consistent prayer for your leaders and their families
- Public acknowledgement to the broader church body of their dedication
- Provide free or low-cost outings, fellowships, and dinners for them
- Send cards of encouragement, thanks, and gratitude throughout the year
- Give gifts of appreciation; even small things mean a lot

TIP

Encouragement is a lot like communication. It's tough to offer too much of it!

WHAT AN URBAN YOUTH MINISTRY LEADER IS NOT

When leading an urban youth ministry, I don't have to:

- know every little detail of what's going on in the ministry at all times.
- have specific training and certification or feel the pressure to teach every aspect of the Bible all the time.
- feel as if I'm going to be needed *all the time*!
- come across as some cool, hip young person who looks just like the students do.

- commit all of my free time to the ministry.
- be wild, crazy, dynamic, tell jokes, facilitate games, and turn flips.
- be liked by all the students and parents.
- command respect from all of the students, parents, and church; if I'm living right and loving students, respect will come.
- be a part of a "clique" or "social club" at the church.

Urban ministry isn't easy, and it's not always comfortable. However, with prayer, commitment, faith, and dedication, God will begin to bless you indeed and enlarge your territory. Your confidence will develop and grow as time goes on and as you grow in your experience. God can and does use ordinary people to do extraordinary things!

THE PROGRAMS

Take time to identify your "target audience." What teenagers are you ministering to? Who do you want to consider reaching that you may not currently have in your plans? It's important to do this first before you create your programs because this will affect the relevance and impact of your ministry. Once you've identified your target audience, you can begin to build your programs. In his book *Purpose-Driven Youth Ministry* (available through simplyyouthministry.com), Doug Fields talks about how you must first identify the audience you are targeting before you can develop an effective youth program. Here are five "types of students" based on Fields' book.

TIP
Programs are designed to serve people; people were not created to simply serve your programs.

1. **The Community Student:** Any unchurched student who lives within a realistic driving distance from your church.

2. **The Casual Fan:** Anyone who attends your weekly worship services. These teenagers make up your regular attendees and include both Christians and non-Christians.

3. **The Season Ticket Holder:** Anyone who gets involved in your youth services, Bible classes, or small groups. These students are Christians who want to connect with other Christians and desire to grow in their faith.

4. **The Player:** These students are growing through developing spiritual habits and disciplines such as personal Bible study, prayer, accountability with other Christians, Scripture memorization, and giving (tithe). These teenagers show an understanding and expression of evangelism, and want to reach their friends for Christ.

5. **The Starting Lineup:** These are the committed students who have discussed and discovered their gifts, are serving in a ministry, and are actively reaching their friends for Christ.

The goal and focus: Know your potential audience and find ways to lead them from being a community student to being in the starting lineup.

Too often we develop youth programs that are relevant and meaningful to "us" but not for the students that are in our surrounding communities, local schools, or within our churches. When you are thinking through how you want to develop your program and what type of flavor or DNA you want your youth ministry to have, it's important that you keep this programming equation in mind. Before you develop a program, you have to know what your ministry purpose is and who the students your ministry will be serving are.

Potential Student Audience + Purpose = Program
(It's important to identify your students before you design your program)

Why identify your students?
- So you don't develop programs for students that don't exist
- So you don't generalize your expectations of all students
- Because one program cannot effectively reach all levels of student commitments

Now that your audience is identified, you can begin developing your program. What follows is a "menu" of program ideas and descriptions that I've used at Peace Baptist Church that you may consider adapting and using in your ministry:

Student Care Given for Crisis

Unless you are a certified and licensed counselor, you cannot offer "counseling" to students. Student Care Given for Crisis is a ministry designed to set up systems of accountability, direction, and help for students with all kinds of family, emotional, physical or mental challenges. Partner with local social service agencies and develop a referral system to help navigate students who are going through various challenging situations. This can be set up by having a hotline, e-mail address, or weekly office time.

Basic Training Classes

- Membership
- Maturity
- Ministry
- Missions

Basic Training is a membership-to-mission process used to develop and train students in basic biblical and spiritual principles, and an opportunity to teach them how to study, understand, and articulate God's Word.

Impact Cell Groups

Impact Cell Groups (small groups) are weekly co-ed Bible studies geared toward handling life's issues based on the Word of God. Issues include such topics as sexuality, drugs, pornography, depression, low self-esteem, and peer pressure.

Men of Distinction

Men of Distinction is a monthly mentoring and training time for young men ages 13-18 to be strong, stable, positive, and successful spiritually, emotionally, socially, and physically. It is a

TIP

Main youth services have dynamic energy, but a vibrant small group ministry is a powerful way to produce changed lives!

"rites of passage" ministry designed to help teenage boys develop into authentic men of God.

Women of Virtue

Women of Virtue is a monthly ministry focused on the development of young women's purity and virtue. It explores the true essence of their beauty and self-worth, as found in God's design. Cultural outings, makeovers, self-esteem training, workshops, seminars, and fashion expositions are just a few of the events.

Pregnancy Care Support

Pregnancy Care Support is a ministry to offer support and a sense of hope to teenage mothers. This ministry is a place of restoration, healing, strength, and help.

Performance Arts Ministry

This innovative ministry consists of Christ-centered, artistically talented young Christians who serve as warriors for God and ambassadors of the performing arts, exalting the name of Jesus. The goal of this ministry is to unlock and release hidden or suppressed talents so these gifts can be nurtured, developed, and used to minister to this generation. The performance arts ministry participates in student worship services.

David's Dance

This group of young men and women is anointed to dance and give glory and honor to Jesus Christ. The purpose is to bring dance back to the church as God originally ordained it and as David spoke of it. These students perform praise dance, interpretive dance, and liturgical dance.

GΦG (Glory Phi God) Step Team

This ministry impacts students both within and outside of the church with innovative methods of expression that all students can relate to. This expression is an effort to empower, inspire, and maintain involvement in the church.

TIP

This ministry was birthed out of a need in our own community. What needs in your community can your youth ministry help meet?

NXL: Next Level

This ministry is for our young adults ages 18-26. It is a ministry that assists in the development and transition to the next level of life in the adult world and in Christ. This group meets during Wednesday Bible study hour and on two Saturdays a month for Saturday Night Live Worship.

The UNIT: Student Leadership Team

This group of teenagers serves as the youth council of the ministry. They are responsible for maintaining the proper communication with the students, parents, and governing church body. They plan events and special functions that will encourage the highest level of youth participation. The ministerial arm of this group is involved in various outreach activities and mission activities.

The CORE: Student Prayer Team

Our student prayer warriors meet weekly for effective and fervent prayer. These students are interceding on behalf of our church, schools, city, state, government, and nation.

"My School" Campus Ministry

This ministry goes right into the local mission field of the school campuses. Weekly Bible studies, prayer services, and devotions take place at various local middle schools and high schools.

Student Recovery Group

This program is designed to help students heal from life's hurts, habits, and hang-ups. It's a real, live class that deals with real-life issues. This small group sees itself as a hospital for the hurting.

Parent Church Association (PCA)

This monthly ministry is designed to bridge the gap in parent-student relations. This group of parents serves as the advisory board to the youth department. They oversee field trips, fundraisers, chaperone schedules, and class volunteers.

TIP
Prayer is another one of those things that you can't do too much. Pray for your students! Pray for your pastor! Pray for your families! Pray for God's work in your youth ministry!

LifeLine Student Worship Service

This is a time to see the power of God and most of the ministries within the youth department in action. Services include high-energy stepping, rapping, praise and worship, poetic moments, skits, plays, and interactive messages.

Adopt-A-Block

This monthly event is a time to teach students the importance of giving back and helping within the community. The Adopt-A-Block ministry serves the community in various ways such as lawn care, dumping and cleaning trash, feeding the homeless (soup kitchen), painting, and giving attention to any other needed area within the surrounding community.

These are just a few examples of the different types of programs you can have within your urban youth ministry. The important thing is to keep students inspired and engaged. However, you don't want to over-commit and under-deliver. Discover what works best for you and stay in your lane. Don't try to be something you're not, because urban students will see right through you and you will lose credibility and authenticity quickly. The best youth ministries, no matter what the culture or demographics, are the ones that are God-inspired and student-led!

TIP

Get out and serve your community. Your students' lives will be changed as they take on the role of servant leaders.

Goals and objectives are "strategic indicators" that enable you to track the progress of your ministry as you move toward your God-given vision. They allow you to measure key growth factors and continually improve the quality of programming. They also assist you as you set your priorities. What are your "must have" goals, what are your "nice to have" goals, and what are your "postpone until next year" goals?

Quantitative goals and objectives

Quantitative goals provide a tangible way for you to measure the progress of your ministry vision by establishing numerical targets for key growth areas. What will you need "more" of in the future to achieve your God-given vision? Will you need more attendance, leaders, finances, participation, group interaction, classes, activities, teachers, space, or equipment? How much or how many more?

To properly set these types of goals, begin by establishing an ultimate target that can be identified numerically. Once you do that, then you can effectively track your progress on a weekly, monthly, quarterly, or annual basis to determine your progress.

Qualitative goals and objectives

Qualitative goals and objectives represent the "quality" of the ministry by identifying how you can make it "better." Often the measurement used for these types of goals will emerge through interviews with students and parents, surveys about how students felt about a program or event, or other "soft" or informal methods of examining program effectiveness. How can you improve the quality of the programming, leadership, attendance, marketing, curriculum, and experience? What spiritual impact is your youth ministry having?

Although qualitative goals are harder to measure and seem "intangible," you can track your progress by using a process of quantification. Quantification occurs when you establish good or bad extremes on a sliding scale of +10 to −10. By identifying your

TIP

If you can't accomplish every goal this year, relax. Pray for God's direction and guidance on what his priorities are for your ministry.

ultimate target, you can quantify how well you are doing as you move toward your ultimate goal or objective.

Examples of qualitative goals

1. We want to develop a training program for adults and student leaders who are called to our youth ministry; we want to develop and train a team that believes in the importance of investing in the lives of students.
   - Offering monthly leadership training session meetings
   - Providing quarterly spiritual gifts workshops to help people find their place in ministry
   - Recruiting adults and students who show potential of being great leaders within the ministry and have a positive influence
   - Using Doug Fields' *Purpose-Driven Youth Ministry* and other relevant training for our leaders

2. We want to provide opportunities for students to participate in corporate worship.
   - Incorporating adult worship leaders and bands in youth events and programs
   - Adding times of worship to our weekly, monthly, and annual calendars
   - Setting up opportunities for parents to worship with their students

3. We want to empower students to have a spirit of entrepreneurship.
   - Exposing them to a variety of business workshops and seminars
   - Teaching them how to develop business plans and proposals
   - Developing a business within the student ministry that is solely run by the students

4. We want to provide parents more opportunities to get involved in the lives of their teenagers.
  - Developing a newsletter geared specifically toward parents
  - Adding a parent training to our quarterly training plan
  - Holding joint meetings between the Youth Council and the Parent Council
  - Setting up mother/son and father/daughter activities

Examples of quantitative goals

1. We want to establish and promote our student worship services (for junior high on Sundays and senior high on Wednesdays), market our new Youth Christian Education Ministry (tutorials and discipleship program), build better relationships and partnerships with the business community, and strengthen our campus ministries programs.
  - Developing effective marketing and promotion— advertisement, radio spots, TV broadcast, T-shirts, hats, posters, brochures, and website development
  - Providing a variety of activities during our midweek programs, small groups, campus ministries, and student worship to truly captivate students
  - Planning events and retreats that will draw students into weekly involvement
  - Increasing our number of adult leaders and parental involvement with the goal of building lasting relationships with students
  - Measuring the results after each quarterly event to check if we reached our targets

2. We want to increase our weekly leadership team by adding at least eight adults this year.
  - Taking potential leaders to lunch on a regular basis
  - Having times together at the youth pastor's home
  - Providing opportunities for the church to see what is happening within the student ministry

TIP

Our goal was to add eight more adults. You may need one or two more—or you may need 20 more!

- Praying for adults who have a heart, love, and passion for student ministry
- Exposing leaders to other student ministries to network people
- Measuring the results each quarter and adjusting our methods

3. We want to grow our youth ministry attendance by 50 percent through evangelism this year.
   - Providing evangelism training for all interested and mature students
   - Equipping students to tell their personal testimony
   - Helping students explore their "sphere of influence" to identify their friends, family members, and members of their community who aren't yet Christians
   - Measuring the results each quarter and tweaking the methods

4. We want to increase student and adult leader participation in spiritual disciplines by 25 percent this year.
   - Taking a survey of the youth group and leaders to see who currently participates in which spiritual disciplines
   - Developing a teaching series on spiritual disciplines
   - Developing (or buying) a small group curriculum on spiritual disciplines
   - Helping students and leaders explore their "sphere of influence" to identify their friends, family members, and members of their community who aren't yet Christians
   - Measuring the results mid-year and at year's end to see if we reached our goal

TIP

Spiritual disciplines are tools for encouraging personal spiritual growth. They are not gauges for ranking which leader is the most spiritual based on how much they do certain things. That was the trap the Pharisees fell into.

You may use other words to describe it, but marketing is an important element to the success of a healthy urban youth ministry. If God is doing incredible things in your teenagers' lives, why wouldn't you want the whole world to know? Get the word out and connect with people who can grow and thrive in your youth ministry!

One of the biggest mistakes people make when marketing a ministry is attempting to be all things to all people. It just doesn't work. Your ministry has a unique vibe and flavor that won't appeal to every teenager in town—and that's OK. Be who God made you to be. Why do you exist? Which teenagers are you already reaching—and which teenagers do you believe God wants you to attract and reach? What does your ministry stand for? How are you making a difference?

Define who you are, and determine the ways your ministry is relevant to your target audience. Look for ways to be fresh, new, and different—but stay true to yourself. As you define your target audience, remember that you're attempting to *attract* people, not *pursue* them. It's a subtle but important difference. An attractive environment and marketing strategy is appealing; an overly aggressive or desperate strategy will push teenagers away from your ministry. Know their world so you will be more effective when you're trying to enter it.

You have more than one audience

Here's an important note: You have multiple target audiences. Current members of your youth group are one audience. Teenagers in the community who don't know Jesus are an audience. Your students' parents are a different audience. Church leaders are yet another audience. Keep this in mind when you market and promote your youth ministry, because something that hits home with a 15-year-old unchurched guy might not go over as well with the 75-year-old grandma in your church—and vice versa. Yet both of them are important people to your youth ministry!

TIP

Personal testimonies remain one of the most powerful tools for marketing and promoting a ministry. Who can argue with a changed life?

TIP

If it helps, think of marketing as another word for "public relations." It's about presenting the story of who you are and why people should care about your ministry.

Is any single audience your most vital? Maybe the best way to answer that question is to remember that your audiences are *different*. I'm most concerned about helping you connect with your audiences of teenagers—students who are currently involved, students who could become involved, and unchurched young people in your community. But as you think about marketing, always be aware of the bigger picture and the multiple audiences that have a stake in your youth ministry.

Are marketing and communicating the same thing?

Any time you communicate with one of your audiences, you're marketing your ministry—and every time you market your ministry, you should be communicating with one of your audiences. What do I mean by this? Let me break it down.

Sometimes marketing is mostly about getting your name into the community. An outreach or community service event is a chance to talk *and* show what matters to your ministry. It creates name recognition and familiarity—even if you don't see an immediate response of people choosing to follow Christ or starting to attend your church. Your communication may not be overt, but you're still communicating an important message to your community.

In some cases, you want to market a message to a specific audience—fliers to middle school students about a basketball tournament or text messages to high school girls about a "girls night out" event. The marketing tool becomes a form of communication. You're informing people about a specific opportunity to connect or get involved.

And other times, your primary activity is communication of an idea, principle, or value—a newsletter to parents talking about tips for investing in their children's lives, a mailer inviting new families in your neighborhood to check out your church, or an e-mail to student leaders challenging them to grow spiritually. You might not see this as "marketing," but that's what you're doing. You're making people aware of the value your ministry adds to their lives—or could add to their lives.

Evaluate your ministry
As a team, take time to examine the barriers for your ministry. Why don't people want to come to your ministry? Don't look at other ministries. Know your own purpose and identity. Take ownership of who you are and what you do best, but also address any issues within your own ministry that might become a hindrance or obstacle to teenagers.

Determine which students are the key influencers on your leadership team and in your youth group. Find ways to inspire and motivate them to take the lead in spreading the word about your youth ministry. Tap into their creativity and ideas on connecting with other teenagers in your community.

Know your overt benefits. What's in it for the individual student who decides to visit your youth ministry? Develop your meaningful difference. Why is it worth it? Why should a teenager take the time to attend, connect, or learn more? Show your real reason to believe. Why should students believe what you're telling them?

Pause for a moment and list some of the benefits of a teenager checking out your youth ministry.

Remember, people move through a step-by-step process as they learn about your youth ministry—and as they move closer to making a commitment to following Jesus. They usually start by being disengaged spectators, then move to spiritually curious, then become seekers, then turn into "public square" Christ-followers, and then have the chance to become "kingdom builders." People want to relate, connect, and be themselves. You've probably heard this saying before, and it's true: People don't care how much you know until they see how much you care.

Four principles for effective marketing

1. Communicate something

Students want to get it the first time. Have something to say. Use leadership students to test the market. They're your first line of communication. Tap into their networks of communication, such as text messages or their online networking accounts such as Facebook®).

2. Reveal something

Begin with the end in mind. Be clear what you're trying to say. Show or tell your audience something about your ministry. Help people learn something they didn't already know about you and your youth ministry.

3. Help people feel

You want to inspire, motivate, and encourage the soul. Speak more to the emotion than to the mind. Find ways to relate to the audience. Use images that cause people to think and respond.

4. Engage your audience

Know your projected ministry personality. Be yourself. Be genuine. Be funny and relevant. Humor opens the door to lowered defenses and a willingness to listen and respond.

MARKETING STRATEGIES

Your target audiences include many groups:

- Late elementary students entering junior high—these are actual and potential future members of your youth group
- Junior high and high school students—these are actual and potential members of your youth group
- College students—these are actual and potential leaders for your youth ministry or members of your young adult ministry

TIP

Engaging your audience will help move people toward a point of connection or learning more about your ministry.

TIP

This isn't a complete list, but these are going to be some of your most important target audiences.

- Parents and legal guardians—these are actual and potential leaders and resources for your youth ministry, and they are influential adults in students' lives
- Students and families who do not know Christ—these are people in your community who may respond as you fulfill the Great Commission
- Students living within realistic driving distance of your church—these are potential members of your youth group
- Church families—these are actual and potential leaders for your youth group and people who can invest time, prayer, and resources in your ministry
- Church leaders—these are people entrusted with the direction of your congregation, and a healthy youth ministry contributes to the overall health of your church

Ways you can advertise and promote:
- T-shirts, hats, jerseys, and other urban wear
- Your church website
- Posters, brochures, and fliers posted in area businesses, schools, and community centers
- Partnerships with other area churches
- School publications, bulletin boards, and announcements
- Mailers
- Newspaper, TV, and radio broadcasts
- Neighborhood outreach and evangelism
- Community calendars and newspaper
- Text messages, Facebook®, and blogs

Ways to communicate with target audiences:
- Brochures
- Posters
- Concert calendar
- Announcements
- Newspaper, TV, and radio announcements
- Community calendars
- Church publications

TIP
Different tools will effectively reach different audiences.

No matter if you are a full-time, part-time, or bi-vocational youth pastor, or a total volunteer, proper time management is essential. No matter what you do, there will always be 24 hours in a day and 7 days in a week. What are you going to do with the time that God has given you? To be an effective leader, you must own your time and not let others dictate your time. It is vital that you have balance in your life, family, and ministry in order for spiritual growth and renewal to take place. Here are a several tips to help you focus on better time management.

1. Look at your daily calendar at the beginning of each day, and make sure that you have enough of a margin between meetings and appointments. Organize, review, or revise your priorities at the beginning of the day.

2. Set a firm deadline for every goal.

3. Don't trust your memory. Carry a pad and jot things down. Take notes at meetings, putting a star by or underlining things that are your responsibility.

4. Be a good steward; make sure each job is done the most economically efficient way.

5. Work to improve your reading skills.

6. Devise a foolproof reminder system, possibly by using your cell phone alarm or setting a reminder in your calendar.

7. Consolidate similar activities, phones calls, correspondence, and other tasks.

8. Meetings are expensive and time-consuming. Give advanced notice of subject matter, keep on target, and respect people's time by finishing at the promised time.

9. Tackle your most demanding tasks during your most productive hours.

TIP

When reading a book, consider keep a pen nearby so you can take notes or mark pages or phrases that impact you.

10. Once a decision has been made—if there is no longer anything you can do about it—let any bad feelings go and move on to your next project.

11. Neatness counts. The philosophy of "a place for everything and everything in its place" is a smart one to follow.

12. Spend some time alone with God each day, even if it is just 15 minutes. Schedule this time if you can. Make it a habit.

13. Be alone to think; some of your best ideas will come when you reflect by yourself.

14. Coordinate activities for an even flow of the work. Spread out deadlines.

15. Learn to say "no" when you should say "no." Don't saddle yourself with any nonessential tasks just to be popular or to keep others happy.

16. Anticipate and plan for your needs and those of others. Don't be a last-minute panic-button pusher.

17. Try to complete each task you tackle without having to come back a second time.

18. If a task is difficult or unpleasant, try to dispose of it as quickly as possible.

19. Put a high value on your minutes and hours. Resolve to get real achievements or real enjoyment out of every waking hour.

20. Get off to an early start. Organize, review, or revise your priorities at the beginning of each day.

TIP

People in ministry have a tough time saying "no." The earlier you can develop this skill, the longer you'll survive and thrive in ministry.

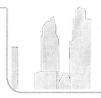
It's important to build and manage your ministry budget. How much does it cost to operate your ministry on an annual basis? It is a great idea to keep track of everything, even materials and/or supplies donated by leaders or one-time volunteers. If you can get your budget under control, your pastor will love you all the more, and you will always know that there is enough budget to meet your ministry's needs. It also may be wise to seek out accountants or financial experts in your church to help you get started.

Annual budget: Develop an annual budget for the department or ministry area. If you have distinct junior high and senior high ministries, you will need to develop a separate budget for each ministry. How much will it cost to operate your ministry for the next 12 months? Be specific. List all of the programs and activities planned for the whole year. It is always a great idea to develop your annual calendar first so you can get a realistic view of all the programs you are trying to fund for the year.

Program/event budget lines: Each program, event, and/or activity within your ministry area will require a separate programming budget (such as VBS, fall outreach or celebration, mission trips, youth conferences, and retreats). When you budget for these areas, be as specific as possible. Go line by line. Here are some examples of things to plan for in each program or event:

1. Food and beverage costs
2. Transportation costs
3. Materials (tablecloths, napkins, and other items)
4. Fees (renting a facility, getting a church membership at a health club, or other fees)
5. Printing and mailing costs (for marketing and promotion)

TIP
Even if you have limited income for your ministry, you still have expenses. It takes resources to effectively minister, and God wants us to be good stewards with the things he has provided.

THE PROGRAMS
CREATING YOUR CALENDARS

Have you ever been guilty of doing the same events every year and just changing out the dates? Do you even know why your church does some of the annual events that are on the calendar? Do your scheduled events coincide with the overall vision and direction of your ministry? Depending on your responses to these questions, you may need to reconsider how and what you are programming every year. Calendaring is so important because it forces you to plan ahead, and it communicates to parents, students, and leaders all of the events and activities within your youth ministry.

When planning youth ministry activities and programs for the year, begin by obtaining a master church calendar. This will give you an overall sense of the "rhythm" of your church and will help you fit into that rhythm. Next, begin developing a calendar for your youth ministry. Divide the year and your calendar into quarters. Plan to meet each month with key leaders for a calendar review and to add any updates to your calendar. After consistently doing this for the first three months, you will be amazed at how easy it is to plan and coordinate your activities.

As you develop your planning calendar, consider creating two types of calendars:

- **Annual Calendar:** a ministry-wide calendar for the entire year
- **Program Calendar:** a calendar that highlights specific programs or events

Here are some calendar samples:

A YEAR AT A GLANCE

Weekly

Wednesday Student Fellowship	Wednesday 6 p.m.
Wednesday Warfare Prayer Service	Wednesday 6:45 p.m.
Impact Small Groups	Wednesday 7 p.m.
Sunday Soldiers Prayer Service	Sunday 8 a.m.

Bible Discovery Hour (Sunday School)	Sunday 11:30 a.m.
Life Hurts, God Heals (student recovery)	Friday 7 p.m.
Campus For Christ (time varies per campus)	
Sunday Student Fellowship (after worship services)	Sunday
Student Worship (every week, except fifth Sunday)	Sunday 9 a.m.

Yearly

Youth Conference	January
Holy Hip-Hop Conference	January
Parent & Guardian Month	February
True Love Waits Conference	February
SYM Conference	March
Student Lock-In	March
Spring Break Retreat	April
Impact Hangout (cultural event)	May
Senior Retreat (graduating 12th-graders)	May
Girlfriends Outreach Retreat	June
Summer Enrichment Program	June
Youth Represent Conference	June
Adventure Trip	July
Mission Trip	August
Back to School Bash	August
Leadership Retreat	September
Donuts with Dads & Muffins with Mom	October
Fall Festival	October
Dinner With Youth Pastor	November
Christmas Party	December
Watch Night Celebration	December

Other Programs

Basic Training	Every 2nd & 4th Sunday
• 101 (Membership)	9:15 a.m.
• 201 (Maturity)	
• 301 (Ministry)	
• 401 (Missions)	
Staff & Leadership Meetings	Monthly
Student Leadership Development	Monthly
Family Nights	Monthly
Tha Spot (young adult worship)	Friday 7 p.m.
Student Impact Enterprise Meeting	1st & 3rd Thursday 7 p.m.
Youth Choir Rehearsal	Saturday 10 a.m.
Men of Distinction Meetings	4th Saturday 9 a.m.
Women of Virtue Meetings	2nd Saturday 9 a.m.
Pregnancy Care Support	Available as needed
Performance Arts Ministry	Rehearsal as needed
• Drama	
• Mime	
• Hip-Hop & Jazz	
• Step	
Youth Department Training	Quarterly

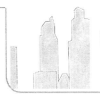

CONCLUSION

Ephesians 2:10 says, *"For we are God's masterpiece. He has created us anew in Christ Jesus, so we can do the good things he planned for us long ago."*

I love the game of football! In my humble opinion, I think it is the ultimate team sport. You have 22 men on the field at one time: 11 on defense and 11 on offense. They all have very different and distinct roles and assignments. Each player on the field has his own unique purpose. The quarterback is often described as the captain of the offense, and usually the middle linebacker calls the defensive plays. Now, if the quarterback and middle linebacker operate outside of their roles and assignments during the game, you will have a huge problem. You will never see a middle linebacker dropping back to throw a pass or a quarterback blitzing the offense and trying to make a tackle behind the line of scrimmage. If you do, you will probably see two talented players being extremely ineffective because they're simply out of place because it's not what their workmanship calls for them to do.

In the same way, God created us by design and with a unique purpose and gift. He dictates to us why we exist. God is the one who gave us our purpose, and he is the one who knows our destiny before we reach it. If we live, operate, or minister outside of our purpose and reason we were created, then we are guaranteed to live a life that is ineffective and void of meaning. Walking in the purpose God has designed for you is how you fulfill your reason for being. You matter to God and students. No matter where you are or if you're getting paid or not, God has created you for this journey you're on. Never strive to be like the ministry next door; be committed to being the ministry God has called you to be. If you try being something you are not, you will only be a cheap copy of a great original.

This manual is designed to help you be the MVP leader God has purposed for you to be and win the Super Bowl for your youth ministry by developing a program that is relevant, inspirational, and driven by design. The next section is filled with all kinds of resources designed to help you in your quest in developing the ideal urban youth ministry. Please feel free to use these resources as your very own. We're in this together! Let's give God our very best!

PART 2
RESOURCES AND TOOLS

CONTENTS

CONTENTS

THE STUDY OF ADOLESCENT DEVELOPMENT

This three-Level chart is designed to help understand where students are in their pre-teen and teen development process. This information can be especially helpful during an adult volunteer training early in the school year to help adults get a better understanding of the teenagers they're working with.

This file can also be found on the CD-ROM:
Part 2 > 1_Real Talk > The Study of Adolescent Development.doc

According to kidsgrowth.com, pre-teens and teenagers develop in three phases:

LEVEL I
Early Adolescence (12-13 years old)

Physical
- Changes are rapid and dramatic
- Stamina is lacking; tiredness and short attention span are common
- Awkward moments are frequent; hands and feet are large in proportion to rest of body
- Begins to show physical signs of sexual maturation; emergence of secondary sexual characteristics
- Girls are usually more mature than boys, entering puberty up to two years earlier
- Most have seemingly superhuman appetites

Emotional
- Begins to develop personal identity and sense of self
- Self-conscious and egocentric, but gaining more confidence
- Enthusiastic
- Dependent on parents, but desire for independence is increasing
- Fluctuates between friendly and moody
- Expresses a positive sense of humor

Social
- Places great value on same-sex peer acceptance; wants to fit in with crowd
- Looks to attach to a few close friends; often cliquish

- Can be overcritical and have unrealistic expectations
- Begins to be interested in opposite sex; girls develop interests earlier
- Develops crushes and identifies heroes
- Most comfortable in small groups of trusted friends of the same sex

Intellectual

- Wants to see proof; less willing to accept others' beliefs (particularly parents' beliefs)
- Begins to think abstractly, but usually views issues in terms of black-or-white answers; increasingly uses reason and logic
- Enjoys problem solving by looking at alternatives and consequences

Spiritual

- Generally receptive to making a decision about a relationship with Christ
- More able to make genuine commitments
- Develops a more sensitive view of right and wrong
- Usually mirrors parents' spiritual views initially
- Begins to develop personal values
- Responds to needs of others; more aware of social issues

LEVEL II
Middle Adolescence (14-15 years old)

Physical

- Physical changes have slowed for girls; boys may still be changing rapidly
- Advanced development of secondary sexual characteristics
- Develops intense sex drive, particularly males
- Active and energetic
- Tends to experiment with alcohol or drugs

Emotional

- Ability to form personal relationships increases
- Less egocentric; learns how to give sacrificially and receive from others
- Often enjoys arguments
- Feels intense need to separate from parents
- Self-assurance can mask deep-felt insecurities and self-doubts
- Seeks recognition for being good in some activity

Social

- Focus moves from same-sex friendships to opposite-sex friendships; dates in groups
- Stays with established circle of friends
- May join a group with social beliefs or values that differ from parents
- Sometimes rebels against people in authority
- May become very protective of personal possessions

Intellectual

- Becomes capable of more complex and abstract thoughts
- Can ask deep questions
- Often questions illogical arguments
- More analytical and critical about belief systems

Spiritual

- Searches for what the Bible says about what is or isn't OK
- May experience guilt about relationships with or thoughts about opposite sex
- May experience frustration with desire to stop some behavior and the apparent inability to do so (such as struggles with pornography or masturbation)
- Often prays for forgiveness

LEVEL III
Late Adolescence (16-18 years old)

Physical

- Physique is almost fully developed
- Boys have caught up with girls developmentally
- Majority have reached adult height
- Expresses a strong interest in personal health
- May fall victim to eating disorders
- Some are sexually experienced

Emotional

- Feels confidence and security with own identity
- Sometimes sentimental
- Can put others' needs ahead of their own
- Recognizes the need to take more personal responsibility
- Usually friendly toward family

Social

- Desires meaningful relationship with others, including opposite sex
- Dating is frequent
- Personal relationships show increasing commitment; many date one partner exclusively
- Driver's license and graduation will be rites of passage
- Many work part time, resulting in discretionary income

Intellectual

- Becomes increasingly involved with future
- Begins to focus on career choices
- Recognizes that current decisions influence future
- Develops ability to consider many options at once; can process possibilities
- Makes better and more mature decisions
- Might be able to resolve conflicts with judgment

Spiritual

- Shows ability to demonstrate strong commitment to a relationship with Christ
- Moral and spiritual values are tested and challenged
- Understands and cares about how others feel and think
- Becomes interested in life after death
- Asks questions and expresses doubts about their spiritual life, such as assurance of salvation
- Is increasingly able to apply spiritual principles to life, and is able to grasp deeper spiritual concepts

ORGANIZATION CHART

The sample organization chart on the next page can be used as a base to help provide structure to a youth ministry team. Your organization chart may not have the same ministries or look like this at all, and that's OK. Also, be aware that the majority of these areas are overseen by a volunteer, not the youth pastor.

This file can also be found on the CD-ROM:
Part 2 > 2_Getting Started > Sample Organization Chart.doc

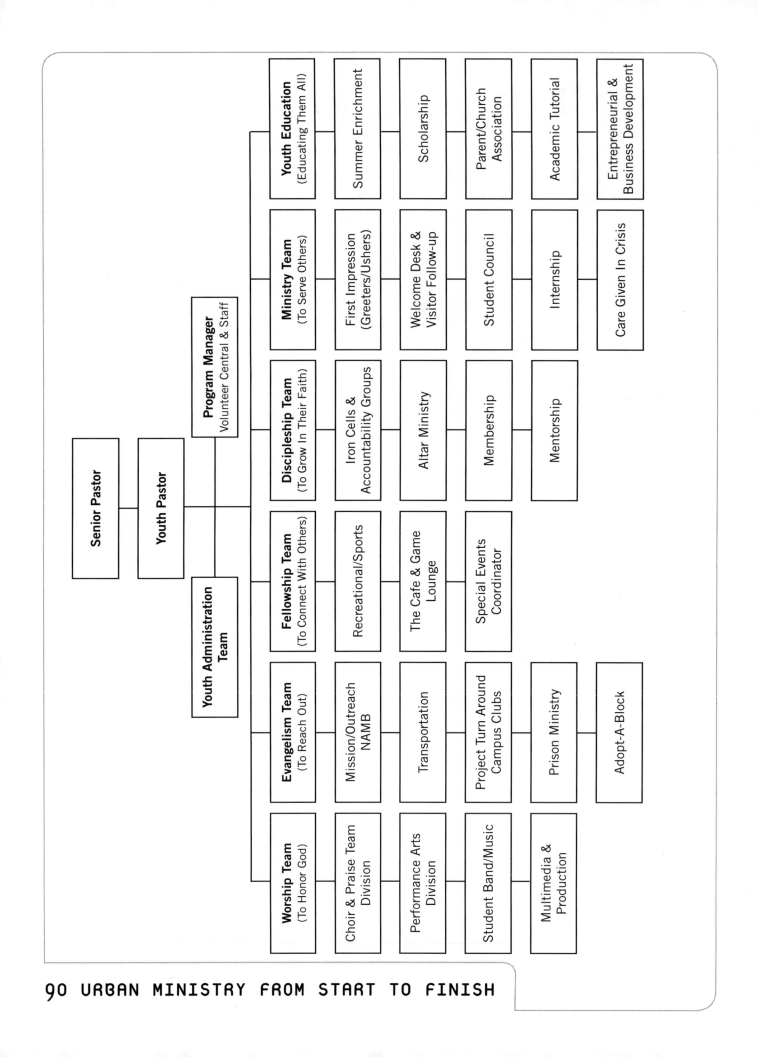

Senior Pastor

Youth Pastor

Youth Administration Team

Program Manager
Volunteer Central & Staff

Worship Team
(To Honor God)

- Choir & Praise Team Division
- Performance Arts Division
- Student Band/Music
- Multimedia & Production

Evangelism Team
(To Reach Out)

- Mission/Outreach NAMB
- Transportation
- Project Turn Around Campus Clubs
- Prison Ministry
- Adopt-A-Block

Fellowship Team
(To Connect With Others)

- Recreational/Sports
- The Cafe & Game Lounge
- Special Events Coordinator

Discipleship Team
(To Grow In Their Faith)

- Iron Cells & Accountability Groups
- Altar Ministry
- Membership
- Mentorship

Ministry Team
(To Serve Others)

- First Impression (Greeters/Ushers)
- Welcome Desk & Visitor Follow-up
- Student Council
- Internship
- Care Given In Crisis

Youth Education
(Educating Them All)

- Summer Enrichment
- Scholarship
- Parent/Church Association
- Academic Tutorial
- Entrepreneurial & Business Development

VISION AND MISSION STATEMENTS

In the development of any organization, vision and mission statements provide a foundation for building a leadership structure. They serve as a blueprint to your program. These statements offer current and future leaders a clear snapshot of your ministry, its direction, and its potential target audiences. In structuring your urban youth ministry, your vision and mission statements are vital. Get a head start on putting together or revising your vision and mission statements using the sample below. Run it by your senior pastor to make sure you're on the same page and sending a unified message to parents, leaders, and your students.

This file can also be found on the CD-ROM:
Part 2 > 2_Getting Started > Sample Vision and Mission Statement.doc

SAMPLE VISION STATEMENT
(Peace Baptist Church Student Ministry Vision Statement)

We envision the Student Impact of Peace Baptist Church being a spiritual organization designed to liberate and empower students to move from living apart from Christ, to serve Christ with all of their heart and soul, and to share him with others. Student Impact will be a place for students to **BELIEVE** in themselves and the power of God and his Spirit; to **BELONG** to something positive, inspirational, and life-changing; and to **BECOME** a Spirit-filled beacon of light in a dark and dismal world. It is our desire to expose both the churched and un-churched student to the true gospel of Jesus Christ, to help them experience the unconditional love of God, and to equip them to serve and share Christ with everyone they come in contact with.

The driving force behind Student Impact is not based on programs, personalities, or gimmicks, but the eternal purpose of God. Our objective is to share Christ and our faith without fear, build and establish relationships that will never fade, and offer students a sense of hope and comfort in times when they feel hopeless. Our focus is to target any unchurched student and move them to becoming a core, committed student who has discovered his or her spiritual gifts, is serving in a ministry, and shows an understanding of prayer, the Word of God, outreach and evangelism, and missions.

SAMPLE MISSION STATEMENT
(Peace Baptist Church Student Ministry Mission Statement)

Our mission is to **REACH** lost students for Christ **(EVANGELISM)**, **RECONNECT** Christian students with other believers **(FELLOWSHIP)**, help students **RENEW** their faith in God **(DISCIPLESHIP)**, inspire them to **RECYCLE** the gifts God has given them **(MINISTRY)**, and **RESTORE** their lives by teaching them to honor God **(WORSHIP)**.

OUR MISSION STATEMENT'S EXPLANATION

Evangelism: Our mission is to encourage students to **REACH** out to unchurched students and share their faith without fear. God has commissioned us to *"Go and make disciples"* *(Matthew 28:19)*.

Fellowship: Our mission is to promote within our student ministry a spirit of unity. In doing so, students weekly **RECONNECT** with other Christian students and believers.

Discipleship: Our mission is to inspire students to develop a deeper walk with Christ by teaching them how to daily **RENEW** their faith and study God's Word. God has commissioned us to *"Teach these new disciples to obey"* *(Matthew 28:20)*.

Ministry: Our mission is to teach students to **RECYCLE** their God-given talents and gifts for the advancement of the kingdom of God. God has commissioned us to *"Love your neighbor as yourself"* *(Matthew 22:39)*.

Worship: Our mission is to teach students how to be **RESTORED** by loving and honoring God with all of their heart and soul in both the personal and private times of their lives. The Great Commandment says, *"You must love the Lord your God with all your heart, all your soul, and all your mind"* *(Matthew 22:37)*.

CORE MINISTRY VALUES

Your core ministry values drive your ministry. It will help you find the right adult or student leaders, define which programs and events are truly worthwhile for your ministry, and also establish a set of standards for your ministry to operate by. Take a look at some of the core values below. Before you put together your list of core values, consider talking with your senior pastor to get his her perception of what your core values should be. Also, consider sitting down with a few of your key adult or student leaders to get their take as well.

This file can also be found on the CD-ROM:
Part 2 > 2_Getting Started > Sample Core Ministry Values.doc

AS LEADERS IN THIS STUDENT MINISTRY WE WILL VALUE...

1. **PRAYER:** We value **PRAYER** because it changes things, confirms our vision, cleanses our hearts, and increases our closeness with God.

2. **WORSHIP:** We value **WORSHIP** because it exalts Jesus and edifies individual Christians and the whole body of Christ.

3. **STEWARDSHIP:** We value **STEWARDSHIP** because every Christian should be committed to a life of biblical stewardship, which involves the use of time, talent, and tithe.

4. **GOD'S WORD:** We value **GOD'S WORD** because it equips, encourages, empowers, and inspires us.

5. **EVANGELISM:** We value **EVANGELISM** because Christians should be the salt of the earth and light to people who don't know Jesus, and we should have an effective witness of Christ's love, forgiveness, and reconciliation.

6. **DISCIPLESHIP:** We value **DISCIPLESHIP** because it is our way of further developing and training Christians for continuous work for God's kingdom.

7. **UNITY:** We value **UNITY** because it strengthens our witness, fellowship, and ability to endure trials, tribulations, and troubles.

8. COMMITMENT: We value **COMMITMENT** because it exemplifies belief and loyalty in the vision and mission of our church as a whole.

9. FELLOWSHIP: We value **FELLOWSHIP** because it promotes unity and community within the body of Christ.

10. EXCELLENCE: We value **EXCELLENCE** because God is excellent and he is worthy of our very best in all we do, what we say, and how we live.

CHARACTER COVENANTS

Setting yourself up with the right adult leaders can help ensure a better youth ministry experience for your students. Having an older, not-so-cool leader in place with the right character qualities instead of younger, immature leader will help you care for your students better, and probably save you a trip or two to your senior pastor's office. Consider some of the character qualities below as you put together your list of character covenants.

This file can also be found on the CD-ROM:
Part 2 > 2_Getting Started > Sample Character Covenants.doc

1. **Christ-likeness:** We resolve to live as Christ would have us live. We will endeavor to hate what is evil, cling to what is good, and to live as those who are accountable to God first. *So we are Christ's ambassadors; God is making his appeal through us. We speak for Christ when we plead, "Come back to God!" (2 Corinthians 5:20).*

2. **Loyalty:** We resolve to be loyal to one another. We will speak well of each other, stick together in tough times, and believe the best of each other as we serve God and others.

3. **Confidentiality:** We resolve to maintain confidentiality in our interactions with the youth, young adults, and one another. We will make a conscious effort to model a professional code of ministerial ethics regarding honesty in self-disclosure.

4. **Growth:** We resolve to continue to grow in the grace and knowledge of Jesus Christ through regular participation in private and corporate prayer, worship, Sunday Impact classes, and Wednesday Night Live discipleship classes.

5. **Training:** We resolve to take part in ongoing education and training activities, conferences, workshops, and seminars. We will continually strive to sharpen our spiritual gifts in order to improve our leadership effectiveness and influence.

6. **Safe Environment:** We resolve to provide our children and teenagers with the safest environment possible—an environment that protects them from pedophiles, rapists, molesters, pornography, drugs, alcohol, inappropriate relationships, and other harmful or immoral influences. In doing so, *all* Youth Development leaders *must* have a criminal background check done in order to work in the Youth Development Department.

7. **Communication:** We resolve to communicate clearly with one another. We will do our best to maintain clear lines of communication and to coordinate all activities.

8. Conflict: We resolve to handle conflicts in a Christ-like manner. We will avoid being overly sensitive or defensive and will deal with conflicts quickly and respectfully.

9. Creativity: We resolve to be creative in our attempts to provide programs, ministries, and activities that are relevant, life-changing, and current with the youth culture. We must not think out of the box—we must think beyond the box.

10. Hardship: We resolve to endure hardship as we work together for the cause of Christ. We will work together to encourage one another and lift one another up during times of personal and corporate difficulty.

STUDENT LEADER EXPECTATIONS

Communicating your expectations in the beginning can save you a lot of time and heartache in the future. Below is a sample student leader expectations form that can help you set the tone of what it means to be a student leader right from the start.

This file can also be found on the CD-ROM:
Part 2 > 3_The People > Sample Student Leader Expectations.doc

This is an opportunity for you as a student to participate in and be responsible for one or more parts of this event or program. While serving in any of the ministry's activities, you will be expected to follow certain guidelines and rules. These guidelines are for your own good, as well as for the overall good of the student ministry. By signing this list of expectations, you are committing to live up to each standard, and you are committing to be held accountable for living a life that is holy and acceptable to Christ. If any leader finds you not living up to any of these expectations, you will be asked and expected to correct the problem. If the problem continues, then you will be sent home at your parent(s)' expense (if necessary), and if it continues thereafter, you will need to be accompanied by your parent(s)' during all student activities in which you are involved.

I, _____, agree to the following:

- I will not swear or use any inappropriate language. I will not use any drugs, tobacco, alcohol, or other inappropriate substances.
- I will only be able to use CD players and iPods at certain times, regulated by leaders. My musical choices will honor God. Leaders have the right to confiscate devices containing any inappropriate music and return them whenever they feel necessary.
- I will only wear appropriate clothing with logos and symbols that are not offensive or negative in meaning. I will not wear pants that sag (guys), and I will not wear tight-fitted clothing or clothing that reveals my belly button, cleavage, or lower back (girls).
- I will not make fun of anyone or make anyone feel less than what God says they are. My words will build up, edify, encourage, and inspire others, not tear them down.
- I will be where I am supposed to be at all times, and I will be on time for everything to the best of my ability.
- I will not partake in any inappropriate public or private affection, sexual activities, or any other physical activities that are contrary to God's Word.

- I will respect others, all leaders, and adults at all times.
- I will not bring, purchase, or view any questionable books, magazines, or websites.
- I will not complain. I understand that all decisions will be made for the good of the group, not an individual.
- I will have a great attitude toward the activities, trips, retreats, and other events.
- I will always work toward having fun, living life to the fullest, and practicing safety.

I agree to live up to these expectations on all church activities.

Student Signature: _____

Date: _____

I understand that my student is responsible for holding to these expectations, and I have reviewed and understand the consequences if he or she does not.

Parent Signature: _____

Date: _____

ADULT LEADER EXPECTATIONS

Communicating your expectations in the beginning can save you a lot of time and heartache in the future. Below is an adult leader expectations form that can help you set the tone of what it means to be an adult leader right from the start.

This file can also be found on the CD-ROM:
Part 2 > 3_The People > Sample Adult Leader Expectations.doc

Thank you so much for your decision to invest in the lives of our students. Your task is not an easy one, but with God's help, together we can build relationships that will last a lifetime with our students, as they develop into Christian adults and leaders. We want this to be an encouraging opportunity for both you and the students; this is why we have created this list of leadership expectations.

I, _____ commit to the following expectations:

- I have given my whole life to Christ.
- Through my talk and my life, I will conduct myself in a manner that represents Jesus Christ.
- I am pursuing and will continue to pursue personal growth in my walk with Christ in this local church body.
- I understand the importance of discipleship and my role as a leader in this ministry.
- I will live a pure, holy, and acceptable life before God and before all whom I encounter. This means that I will not participate in or practice infidelity, pornography, or other compromising lifestyle behaviors that may destroy my witness.
- I will not date, flirt, go out with, or have sexual relationships or any other inappropriate relationships with ANY of the students within the student ministry.
- I will not dress inappropriately in my daily life or at student ministry functions.
- I understand the importance of men ministering to guys and women ministering to girls.
- I will not smoke, drink, or use any inappropriate or illegal substances.
- I will not place myself in situations and circumstances that will discredit my witness and ministry to others.
- I will commit to be at leadership meetings, retreats, and trainings.
- I will commit to communicating any times I am unable to be at any meetings, classes, or trainings.

- It is my responsibility to be where I say I'm going to be and do what I say I'm going to do.

I understand that no one is perfect, except Christ, but I also understand that ministry rises and falls on leadership. And because of that fact, I commit to giving my very best all the time, coming short some of the time, and giving excuses none of the time!

Dear brothers and sisters, not many of you should become teachers in the church, for we who teach will be judged more strictly (James 3:1).

Signature: _____

Date: _____

ADULT LEADER INTEREST FORM

Adult volunteers are a key component of a healthy youth ministry. While just having volunteers may be helpful, volunteers serving in areas of their gifting and passion may experience greater effectiveness and joy in their ministry. This form is designed to get a glimpse at where a potential volunteer may be most interested in serving.

This file can also be found on the CD-ROM:
Part 2 > 3_The People > Adult Leader Interest Form.doc

Thank you for your interest in the student ministry. Please take a moment to complete this brief interest form and return to the volunteer coordinator. Our volunteer coordinator will contact you.

_____   _____
Full Name   Today's Date

_____   _____
Phone Number   Alternate Phone Number

_____
E-Mail Address

_____
Occupation

TEAM LEADERS – LEVEL 1
Team leaders, in consultation with the youth pastor, are responsible for designing, implementing, and evaluating strategies that support the respective ministry mission and overall vision of Student Impact.

Please identify your order of preference in leading, with "1" being the most preferred.
____ Discipleship   ____ Worship
____ Evangelism   ____ Program Manager
____ Fellowship   ____ Volunteer Central Liaison
____ Ministry

TEAM LEADERS – LEVEL 2

Level 2 team leaders, in consultation with the Level 1 team leader, are responsible for designing, implementing, and evaluating strategies that support the respective ministry mission and overall vision of Student Impact.

Team members are responsible for supporting the respective ministry in carrying out its mission.

Are you interested in serving as the team leader of the ministry(ies) you selected?
( ) Yes   ( ) No   ( ) Maybe

Please identify your order of preference, with "1" being the most preferred.

WORSHIP
____ Choir and Praise
____ Drama Ministry
____ Rap Ministry
____ Multi-Media Production
____ Student Band
____ Ministry-in-Motion
____ Music Director

MINISTRY
____ First Impressions
____ Greeters & Ushers
____ Visitors & Welcome Desk
____ Congregational/Student Care
____ Student Council

FELLOWSHIP
____ PBC Café and Coffee
____ Recreational/Sports
____ Events

DISCIPLESHIP
____ Accountability Cell Groups
____ Decision Counseling
____ Student Mentorship
____ Membership
____ Programs
    ____ Tutorial Program
    ____ Scholarship
    ____ Away

EVANGELISM
____ Campus for Christ
____ Guest Follow-up

PERMISSION TO CONDUCT A BACKGROUND CHECK

It's crucial that anyone working with your students undergoes a background check to make sure they are fit for working with teenagers. You must obtain permission from the applicant to run the background check prior to submitting the forms. You may find that this is a natural "weeding-out" process to build a volunteer team of those most fit to work with teenagers. For background checks, visit safechurch.com for more information.

This file can also be found on the CD-ROM:
Part 2 > 3_The People > Permission to Conduct a Background Check.doc

PERMISSION TO CONDUCT A BACKGROUND CHECK

(This form authorizes the church to obtain background information and must be completed by the applicant. The church must keep this completed form on file for at least five years after requesting a background check.)

I, the undersigned applicant (also known as "consumer"), authorize *<<INSERT CHURCH NAME HERE>>* through its independent contractor, LexisNexis, to procure background information (also known as a "consumer report and/or investigative consumer report") about me. This report may include my driving history, including any traffic citations; a Social Security number verification; present and former addresses; criminal and civil history/ records; and the state sex offender records.

I understand that I am entitled to a complete copy of any background information report of which I am the subject upon my request to _____
, if such is made within a reasonable time from the date it was produced. I also understand that I may receive a written summary of my rights under the Fair Credit Reporting Act.

Signature: _____

Date: _____

IDENTIFYING INFORMATION FOR BACKGROUND INFORMATION AGENCY (ALSO KNOWN AS "CONSUMER REPORTING AGENCY")

Print Name: _____

First   Middle   Last

Other Names Used (alias, maiden, nickname): _____

Current Address: _____

Street / P. O. Box

Current Address: _____

City   State   ZIP Code County Dates

Former Address: _____

Street / P. O. Box

Former Address: _____

City   State   ZIP Code County Dates

Social Security Number: _____

Daytime Telephone Number: _____

Driver's License Number: _____ State of Issuance: _____

Date of Birth: _____ Gender: _____

SERVICE DESCRIPTION
CAFE MANAGER

For volunteers and student leaders to meet the expectations that you have for them, they must have a thorough understanding of their roles and responsibilities and what standards you have for excellent service within your ministry. The sample service descriptions that you'll find over the next several pages will help you communicate the roles and responsibilities of your volunteers and student leaders clearly.

This file can also be found on the CD-ROM:
Part 2 > 3_The People > Service Descriptions > Cafe Manager.doc

Ministry	Youth
Reports To	Youth Pastor
Duration of Ministry Opportunity	Ongoing

The desire of the student ministry is to have a spiritually grounded, focused, and life-changing ministry that glorifies God. The café manager manages all aspects of Tha BrickHouse Café and is responsible for the overall and day-to-day operation using teen and adult volunteers. The cafe serves as a safe, centralized place for teenagers and young adults to fellowship, serve in ministry, and learn money management, food preparation, and customer service skills.

Responsibilities
- Establishes guidelines and procedures for café operation.
- Plans menu, selects items for sale to the congregation, and determines cost.
- Prepares food and/or oversees food preparation. Ensures food is properly handled and stored.
- Ensures café is open for business during established hours.
- Ensures kitchen is clean after café is closed for the day. Ensures items are properly stored and secured.
- Maintains stock.
- Purchases food, beverages, supplies, and other items and/or plans for the purchase of these items.
- Maintains accurate accounting records, including purchases, reimbursements, and daily account balances.

- Opens cash register and counts cash on hand. Closes out cash register and counts cash at the end of closing. Forwards *Cash Count* record to student ministry administrator no later than Tuesday of each week.
- Recruits for teen and adult volunteers to ensure the café is properly staffed and operated. Submits requests for volunteers to the volunteer coordinator.
- Ensures the café is open and operational during special events as requested by the youth pastor.
- Trains and/or ensures volunteers are properly trained on café operations and responsibilities.
- Conducts inspections for safety, food storage, service, and sanitation. Performs food service evaluations.
- Attends monthly student ministry team member meetings and updates team on ministry activities and action items, upon request.
- Performs other tasks as assigned or needed to ensure an effective ministry.

Knowledge, Skills, Abilities, and Other Characteristics
- Creativity and initiative to organize, manage, and oversee café operations.
- Knowledge of food handling, preparation, and storage.
- Basic budgeting skills to manage financial records.
- Excellent customer service skills to respond to concerns.
- Computer skills to send and receive e-mails.

Special Qualifications
The café manager must have a passion for Christ, a heart to serve, patience, and initiative to ensure the café is managed with excellence.

Special Physical Qualifications
Ability to lift up to 25 pounds.

SERVICE DESCRIPTION
CAFE VOLUNTEER

This file can also be found on the CD-ROM:

Part 2 > 3_The People > Service Descriptions > Cafe Volunteer.doc

Ministry	Youth
Reports To	Cafe Manager
Duration of Ministry Opportunity	Ongoing

The desire of the student ministry is to have a spiritually grounded, focused, and life-changing ministry that brings glory to God. The café volunteer assists the café manager and gains experience in the food and beverage industry, money management, customer relations, and inventory management. The volunteer may serve as a cashier, short order cook, and/or server.

Responsibilities

SHORT ORDER COOK
- Prepares prepackaged foods. Ensures food is properly handled and stored.
- May assist with inventory.
- Assists with cleaning the kitchen after the café is closed for the day. Ensures items are properly stored and secured.
- Performs other tasks as assigned or needed to ensure an effective café operation.

Knowledge, Skills, Abilities, and Other Characteristics
- Knowledge of food handling, preparation, and storage.
- Knowledge of menu items.
- Ability to operate a microwave, electric tabletop grill, and electric or manual can opener.
- Excellent customer service skills to respond to concerns.

CASHIER

- Opens cash register and counts cash on hand/till before opening for business. Closes out cash register and counts cash at the end of closing. Forwards *Cash Count* record to cafe manager before leaving for the day.
- Totals bills and accepts cash (or gift card) from customers when taking food orders and ensures proper change is given.
- Keeps serving counter clean and dry.
- Cleans tables, helps clean kitchen at closing, and helps keep serving areas stocked with supplies.
- May receive food orders and relay to the cook.
- May assist with inventory.
- Performs other tasks as assigned or needed to ensure an effective café operation.

Knowledge, Skills, Abilities, and Other Characteristics

- Knowledge of food handling, preparation, and storage.
- Knowledge of menu items and prices.
- Basic math skills to total prices and count change.
- Excellent customer service skills to respond to concerns.

SERVER

- Greets customers and receives food orders.
- Relays food orders to cook and/or serves the item if readily available. Ensures that the customer has the proper items including napkin, spoon, fork, and so on.
- Ensures that the customer receives the food items he/she paid for.
- Cleans tables, helps clean kitchen at closing, and keeps serving areas stocked with supplies.
- May also serve as a cashier.
- Performs other tasks as assigned or needed to ensure an effective café operation.

Knowledge, Skills, Abilities, and Other Characteristics

- Knowledge of food handling, preparation, and storage.
- Basic math skills to total prices and count change.
- Excellent customer service skills to respond to concerns.

Other

All café volunteers must wash their hands and handle food properly, exercise safety when working in the café area, and report any concerns to the café manager immediately. Under no circumstances shall a café volunteer turn on the stove or operate equipment other than a microwave, tabletop grill, blender, and can opener.

Special Qualifications

The café volunteer must have a passion for Christ, a heart to serve, patience, and initiative to ensure the café is operated with excellence.

Special Physical Qualifications

Ability to lift up to 15 pounds may be required.

SERVICE DESCRIPTION
CHOIR DIRECTOR AND PRAISE TEAM LEADER

This file can also be found on the CD-ROM:

Part 2 > 3_The People > Service Descriptions > Choir Director and Praise Team Leader.doc

Ministry	Youth, Praise and Worship
Reports To	Youth Pastor
Duration of Ministry Opportunity	Ongoing

The desire of the student ministry is to have a spiritually grounded, focused, and life-changing ministry that glorifies God. The choir director and praise team leader is responsible for leading, organizing, planning, and executing contemporary praise and worship during Sunday morning service, Wednesday night service, and special events.

Responsibilities

- Schedules, plans, and leads rehearsals for the active participation of choir and praise team members in Sunday morning worship services and special events. Provides lyrics and special instructions.
- Plans and selects musical selections to be sung by the choir and praise team. Prepares and publishes a monthly music schedule.
- Consults with the youth pastor to plan music selections related to the message or event.
- Sets up microphones and conducts sound checks 30 minutes before service begins and stores microphones at the end of each service.
- Arranges for the choir's and/or praise team's participation in special internal and external ministry events.
- Arranges for special soloists, accompanists, or instrumentalists in consultation with the minister of worship and arts.
- Arranges for and/or purchases music, supplies, materials, and equipment upon budget approval from the youth pastor and/or minister of music and worship.
- Attends meetings required to plan for special events.
- Arranges for backup director (or comparable leadership) during planned or emergency absences.
- Advises on and requests equipment to ensure services are executed efficiently.

- Supervises recruitment and orientation of new choir and praise team members.
- Maintains music library.
- Coordinates with the sound team to ensure equipment is operating properly.
- Provides musical selections and special instructions to the DJ.
- Ensures that the service administrator and DJ are informed of any ministry needs before service begins or changes during service.
- Prepares lyrics using Microsoft PowerPoint to display on screen during service.
- Provides skill training to choir and praise team members.
- Assists the youth pastor and/or minister of music and worship in preparing annual budget.
- Requests and solicits assistance and volunteers to assist with special events as needed.
- Consults with ministry leaders and coordinates musical activities upon requests for the choir and/or praise team to minister.
- Attends monthly student ministry team member meetings and updates team on ministry activities and action items.
- Performs other tasks as assigned or needed to ensure an effective ministry.

Knowledge, Skills, Abilities, and Other Characteristics
- Creativity and initiative to organize, manage, and oversee ministry activities.
- Knowledge of the World Wide Web to research music and other ministry related information.
- Knowledge of PowerPoint to prepare weekly presentation of songs.
- Computer skills to send and receive e-mails.
- Interpersonal skills to encourage high standards of spiritual commitment and musical excellence in participants.

Special Qualifications
The choir director and praise team leader must have a passion for Christ, a heart to serve, an intimate understanding of the relationship to and impact of music on worship, and initiative to ensure the music ministry is executed with excellence.

Special Physical Qualifications
None.

SERVICE DESCRIPTION
CREATIVE TEAM PROJECT LEADER

This file can also be found on the CD-ROM:
Part 2 > 3_The People > Service Descriptions > Creative Team Project Leader.doc

Ministry	Youth
Reports To	Youth Pastor
Duration of Ministry Opportunity	Ongoing

The desire of the student ministry is to have a spiritually grounded, focused, and life-changing ministry that glorifies God. The creative team project leader serves in an ad hoc capacity and is fully responsible for the overall direction and management of one-time projects, ensuring consistency with the vision of the student ministry and the church as a whole.

Responsibilities

- Consults with the youth pastor to determine overall vision, resources, and approach of the project.
- Coordinates all aspects of the project with assistance of teen and adult volunteers, church staff, consultants, and other individuals.
- Leads others in accomplishing specific tasks to ensure the project is developed and delivered on time and under cost.
- Assesses and determines the qualifications required to accomplish the project and recruits for such knowledge, skills, and abilities in consultation with the volunteer coordinator.
- Serves as primary liaison between the youth pastor and creative team.
- Monitors project progress, deliverables, and quality assurance. Manages time and budgets. Initiates action to identify and resolve problems.
- Reports on project; identifies and resolves risks that impact project completion.
- Adjusts resources as necessary to ensure project success and completion.
- Provides direction and feedback to all team members and assists them in resolving problems.
- Provides guidance to team members on administrative and technical problems.
- Empowers team members to plan and execute responsibilities.

- Prepares and delivers formal presentations as needed.
- Leads meetings required to accomplish the project.
- Performs other tasks as assigned or needed to ensure an effective ministry.

Knowledge, Skills, Abilities, and Other Characteristics
- Creativity and initiative to organize, manage, and oversee ad hoc ministry projects.
- Knowledge of project management techniques to manage projects from conception to delivery.
- Computer skills to send and receive e-mails. Knowledge of Microsoft Office to prepare a variety of documents and the World Wide Web to research information.
- Budget skills to maintain, monitor, and reconcile expenses and ensure projects are completed under budget.
- Interpersonal skills to encourage high standards of spiritual commitment and excellence in participants.
- Excellent communication skills, flexibility, high adaptability to changes.
- Effective writing skills to prepare reports and content, relay project information to team members, and other tasks.
- Strong analytical skills to organize and understand information from a variety of inputs.
- Ability to maintain positive and cooperative working relationships.
- Must be broadly focused and able to manage multiple efforts concurrently.

Special Qualifications
The creative team leader must have a passion for Christ, a heart to serve, and strong project management skills.

Special Physical Qualifications
None.

SERVICE DESCRIPTION
DECISION COUNSELOR

This file can also be found on the CD-ROM:

Part 2 > 3_The People > Service Descriptions > Decision Counselor.doc

Ministry	Youth, Discipleship Ministry
Reports To	Youth Pastor
Duration of Ministry Opportunity	Ongoing

The desire of the student ministry is to have a spiritually grounded, focused, and life-changing ministry that glorifies God. The discipleship ministry is responsible for ensuring that teenagers and young adults choosing to follow Christ, rededicating their life, or accepting the call for membership during altar calls appropriately assimilated into the church. The decision counselor:

Responsibilities

- Receives and escorts teenagers and young adults choosing to follow Christ, rededicating their life, or accepting the call for membership during the altar call.
- Ministers to teenagers and young adults during decision counseling—discussing their decision, answering questions, praying with them, and providing instructions on the next steps.
- Ensures that the *Student Record* (or comparable document) is available during decision counseling and properly and fully completed by each student.
- Transfers student's contact information from the *Student Record* to ensure information is readily available. Within 72 hours of a student's decision, contact student to answer any questions, pray for the student, and/or schedule the student for membership class, if required.
- Forwards the *Student Record* to the student ministry administrator at the end of each service to prepare and mail out follow-up correspondence within 48 hours to each teenager or young adult who decided to follow Jesus, rededicated their life, or accepted the call to membership: a postcard for rededications and membership, and a letter for individuals choosing to follow Christ for the first time.
- Notifies the ministry leader of a planned or emergency absence to ensure coverage for receiving teenagers/young adults during altar call and decision counseling.

- Prepares reports (such as number completed membership class) upon request.
- Attends monthly student ministry team member meetings and updates team on ministry activities and action items.
- Performs other tasks as assigned or needed to ensure an effective ministry.

Knowledge, Skills, Abilities, and Other Characteristics
- Knowledge of the "Romans Roadmap to Salvation" or similar outline to use during decision counseling.
- Knowledge of the "Sinner's Prayer" to pray with every student during decision counseling.
- Basic knowledge of Microsoft Word and/or Excel to prepare correspondence and develop and/or maintain lists. Basic knowledge of e-mail to send and receive information.
- Strong organizational skills to follow up with students and transfer information to the student ministry administrator, upon request.
- Strong interpersonal skills to minister to the students during decision counseling.
- Strong verbal skills to present information during decision counseling.

Special Qualifications
Individuals who serve on the decision counseling team of the discipleship ministry must have a passion for Christ, a heart to serve, and a discerning spirit to minister to individual and group needs.

Special Physical Qualifications
None.

SERVICE DESCRIPTION
DISCIPLESHIP MINISTRY LEADER

This file can also be found on the CD-ROM:

Part 2 > 3_The People > Service Descriptions > Discipleship Ministry Leader.doc

Ministry	Youth, Discipleship Ministry
Reports To	Youth Pastor
Duration of Ministry Opportunity	Ongoing

The desire of the student ministry is to have a spiritually grounded, focused, and life-changing ministry that glorifies God. The discipleship ministry is responsible for ensuring that teenagers and young adults choosing to follow Christ, rededicating their life, or accepting the call for membership during altar call are appropriately assimilated into the church. This ministry is responsible for decision counseling, membership, and water baptism.

Responsibilities

DISCIPLESHIP/DECISION COUNSELING
- Oversees a team of teen and adult volunteers ensuring that they are adequately trained concerning decision counseling and to effectively serve in the discipleship ministry.
- Develops procedures and guidelines to ensure an effective and efficient ministry.
- Evaluates and provides feedback for individuals serving in the ministry.
- Receives and escorts teenagers and young adults choosing to follow Christ, rededicating their life, or accepting the call for membership during the altar call. Ensures that a private area is set up and available before service begins.
- Ministers to teenagers and young adults during decision counseling—explaining their decision, answering questions, praying with them, and providing instructions on the next steps.
- Ensures that the *Student Record* (or comparable document) is available during decision counseling. Coordinates with and submits requests to the church's communications administrator to ensure that forms, certificates, and letterhead are available. Requests must be submitted at least 10 days in advance to ensure availability.

- Prepares and mails follow-up correspondence within 48 hours to each teenager or young adult who decided to follow Christ, rededicated their life, or accepted the call to membership: a postcard for rededications and membership, and a letter for individuals choosing to follow Christ for the first time.
- Ensures stamps are available for weekly mailings. Contacts the youth pastor or submits a purchase order or reimbursement request.
- Contacts each student within 72 hours of their decision to answer any questions, pray for the student, and/or schedule them for membership class, if required.
- Abstracts the information from the *Student Record* and e-mails an Excel spreadsheet to the youth administrator for entering into ACS.
- Notifies the service administrator of a planned or emergency absence to ensure someone is prepared to receive the teenagers/young adults during altar call.

MEMBERSHIP
- Prepares materials for and conducts the membership class for teenagers from sixth grade through 18 years old.
- Completes and presents membership certificates.
- Provides students' full name and the month the membership class was completed to the student ministry administrator for inclusion in the monthly student newsletter. This information must be provided no later than the 15th of each month to ensure publication in the upcoming month.
- Ensures a backup to conduct the membership class in case of a planned or emergency absence.
- Consults with the Peace Baptist Church membership ministry to ensure that ministry needs are represented and integrated into the overall vision of the church.
- Performs other tasks as assigned or needed to ensure an effective ministry.

WATER BAPTISM
- Provides the student's name, telephone number, and parent's name to the ministry leader of the baptism ministry for anyone desiring to be baptized. Completion of membership class is required for baptism.
- Follows up with teenagers (sixth grade to 18 years old) who have been baptized and schedules them for the membership class. Occasionally the PBC membership ministry will notify the teen ministry of a teenager being baptized without completing the membership class.
- Provides the full name and the month the baptism was conducted to the student ministry administrator for inclusion in the monthly student newsletter. This information must be provided no later than the 15th of each month to ensure publication in the upcoming month.

OTHER

- Attends monthly student ministry team member meetings and updates team on ministry activities and action items.
- Prepares reports (such as number of students baptized or number completed membership class) upon request.

Knowledge, Skills, Abilities, and Other Characteristics

- Knowledge of the "Romans Roadmap to Salvation" or similar outline to use during decision counseling.
- Knowledge of the "Sinner's Prayer" to pray with every student during decision counseling.
- Basic knowledge of Microsoft Word and/or Excel to prepare correspondence and develop and/or maintain lists. Basic knowledge of e-mail to send and receive information.
- Strong organizational skills to manage program requirements, follow up with students, and transfer information to the baptism ministry and membership ministry, upon request.
- Strong interpersonal skills to minister to the students during decision counseling.
- Strong verbal skills to present information during decision counseling and membership class.
- A thorough knowledge of the *ABC's of Christianity* and other foundational knowledge to present a membership class to teenagers (sixth grade to 18 years old).

Special Qualifications

The discipleship ministry leader must have a passion for Christ, a heart to serve, and a discerning spirit to minister to individual and group needs. He/she must be able to train and manage a team of teen and adult volunteers.

Special Physical Qualifications

None.

SERVICE DESCRIPTION
DISC JOCKEY (DJ)

This file can also be found on the CD-ROM:

Part 2 > 3_The People > Service Descriptions > Disc Jockey.doc

Ministry	Youth, Sound and Lighting
Reports To	Youth Pastor
Duration of Ministry Opportunity	Ongoing

The desire of the student ministry is to have a spiritually grounded, focused, and life-changing music ministry that glorifies God. The DJ plays the appropriate music during the appropriate portion of the Sunday morning service.

Responsibilities

- Maintains continuous music play during the service unless instructed by the pastor or speaker. There should be no dead time/silence unless instructed by the pastor or speaker.
- Upbeat contemporary gospel 15 minutes before and 10 minutes after service starts.
- Countdown to alert others that service is starting soon and/or countdown to alert choir and praise team to get in position.
- Selections provided by the choir/praise team director.
- Upbeat contemporary gospel/or instrumental during offering.
- Instrumental with a medium tempo during announcements. Do not play music with lyrics or talking; it is extremely disruptive to the speaker and the congregation.
- Instrumental, slow tempo music during altar call.
- Upbeat contemporary gospel or instrumentals after benediction (service concludes).
- Ensures that the appropriate music is readily available and played on cue.
- Pays attention to cues provided by the choir/praise team director, pastor, or speaker to ensure that the music flows without interruption.
- Maintains the quality of equipment performance. Adjusts sound consistent with the service.
- Stores CDs and headphones at the conclusion of each service.
- Makes CD compilations for use during service.

- Identifies music for use during service and submits requests to the student ministry administrator.
- Consults with the youth pastor, speaker, choir director, or service coordinator on special music selections.
- Trains and provides guidance to other DJs.
- Assists the service coordinator in "breaking down" and storing equipment (such as projector) at the end of service upon request.
- Performs other tasks as assigned or needed to ensure an effective ministry.

Knowledge, Skills, Abilities, and Other Characteristics
- Knowledge of music equipment (such as sound boards and microphone levels) to ensure equipment is properly connected.
- Knowledge of mixing techniques to ensure there is no "dead time" and a smooth transition from one musical selection to the next musical selection.
- Knowledge of contemporary gospel to identify and select appropriate music for a teen/young adult church service.
- Microphone skills to make announcements, engage the congregation.

Special Qualifications
Individuals who serve as a DJ must be sensitive to the leading of the Holy Spirit and have a passion for Christ, a heart to serve, and initiative to ensure services run smoothly. Individuals must be able to adapt to last-minute changes.

Special Physical Qualifications
None.

SERVICE DESCRIPTION
GREETERS AND USHERS MINISTRY LEADER

This file can also be found on the CD-ROM:

Part 2 > 3_The People > Service Descriptions > Greeters and Ushers Ministry Leader.doc

Ministry	Youth, Greeters and Ushers Ministry
Reports To	Youth Pastor
Duration of Ministry Opportunity	Ongoing

The desire of the student ministry is to have a spiritually grounded, focused, and life-changing ministry that glorifies God. The Greeters and Ushers Ministry works closely with the Visitors and Welcome Desk Team to ensure that members and visitors feel welcome during Sunday morning service and special events and that services flow as smoothly as possible.

Responsibilities
- Oversees the Greeters and Ushers Ministry ensuring that greeters and ushers are available for Sunday morning service, special events, and as requested.
- Provides training and direction to teen/young adult and adult greeters and ushers. Ensures that teenagers and young adults serving in the ministry have a servant's heart and welcoming demeanor.
- Ensures that the teen and adult greeters and ushers are strategically positioned to seat the congregation and minimize walking during service. At a minimum, four ushers should be posted with an adult usher at the back door to minimize walking in and out the sanctuary.
- Ensures that the greeters and ushers hand out visitor cards, surveys, and other items to the congregation.
- Administers Communion. Ensures that Communion is set up and available on the first Sunday of each month. Contacts appropriate person for information on Communion.
- Collects and counts offering. Prepares offering in-take envelope and places the offering envelope in the youth pastor's office for pickup by the church's finance administrator (or designee).
- Collects items (such as surveys) and forwards to the student ministry administrator, youth pastor, or respective ministry leader for action.

- Attends monthly student ministry team member meetings and updates team on ministry activities and action items.
- Assists the ministry leader for the Visitors and Welcome Desk as requested.
- Performs other tasks as assigned or needed to ensure an effective ministry.

Knowledge, Skills, Abilities, and Other Characteristics
- Creativity and initiative to organize, manage, and oversee a ministry.
- Overall knowledge of Peace Baptist Church ministries and facilities to provide information and/or direct visitors to the appropriate location or ministry contact person.
- Initiative to address congregational needs.
- Strong organizational skills to manage program requirements and receive and transfer information to respective ministries.
- Computer skills to send and receive e-mail.

Special Qualifications
Individuals who oversee and/or serve in the greeters and ushers ministry must have a passion for Christ, a heart to serve, and initiative to ensure our congregation's needs are addressed during service time. Individuals responsible for counting the offering must complete a background check. Contact the youth pastor for required forms.

Special Physical Qualifications
Ability to lift up to 15 pounds.

SERVICE DESCRIPTION
GREETERS AND USHERS MINISTRY TEAM MEMBER

This file can also be found on the CD-ROM:

Part 2 > 3_The People > Service Descriptions > Greeters and Ushers Ministry Team Member.doc

Ministry	Youth, Greeters and Ushers Ministry
Reports To	Youth Pastor
Duration of Ministry Opportunity	Ongoing

The desire of the student ministry is to have a spiritually grounded, focused, and life-changing ministry that glorifies God. The Greeters and Ushers Ministry works closely with the Visitors and Welcome Desk team to ensure that members and visitors feel welcome during Sunday morning service and special events and that services flow as smoothly as possible.

Responsibilities
- Ensures that the teen and adult greeters and ushers are strategically positioned to seat the congregation and minimize walking during service. At a minimum, four ushers should be posted with an adult usher at the back door to minimize walking in and out the sanctuary.
- Ensures that greeters and ushers hand out visitor cards, surveys, and other items to congregation.
- Administers Communion. Ensures that Communion is set up and available on the first Sunday of each month.
- Collects and counts offering. Prepares offering in-take envelope and places offering envelope in the youth pastor's office for pickup by the church's finance administrator (or designee).
- Collects items (such as surveys) and forwards to the student ministry administrator, youth pastor, or respective ministry leader for action.
- Attends monthly student ministry team member meetings and updates team on ministry activities and action items.
- Assists the ministry leader for the Visitors and Welcome Desk as requested.
- Performs other tasks as assigned or needed to ensure an effective ministry.

Knowledge, Skills, Abilities, and Other Characteristics
- Overall knowledge of Peace Baptist Church ministries and facilities to provide information and/or direct visitors to the appropriate location or ministry contact person.
- Initiative to address congregational needs.
- Computer skills to send and receive e-mail.

Special Qualifications
Individuals who serve in the greeters and ushers ministry must have a passion for Christ, a heart to serve, and initiative to ensure our congregation's needs are addressed during service time. Individuals responsible for counting the offering must complete a background check. Contact the youth pastor for required forms.

Special Physical Qualifications
Ability to lift up to 15 pounds.

SERVICE DESCRIPTION
SMALL GROUP LEADER

This file can also be found on the CD-ROM:

Part 2 > 3_The People > Service Descriptions > Small Group Leader.doc

Ministry	Youth, Small Groups
Reports To	Small Group Ministry Director
Duration of Ministry Opportunity	Ongoing

The desire of the student ministry is to have a spiritually grounded, focused, and life-changing ministry that glorifies God. The small group leader leads a small group of teenagers or young adults (sixth grade to college age) in the study and application of the Word of God. The teenagers and young adults are separated by grade/age level.

Responsibilities

- Leads a small group on a regular and continuous basis.
- Facilitates group discussions and Bible lessons.
- Maintains an "open chair policy" and receives new students.
- Identifies and recruits co-leader and support positions.
- Provides data to Impact Cell Groups Ministry leader upon request.
- Oversees the small group and ensures that students are assimilated into the group. Promotes and maintains a welcoming atmosphere for new members to the small group.
- Participates in training provided to small group leaders.
- Ensures that critical needs of the group are identified and communicated to church leadership immediately (such as urgent prayer requests).
- Assesses small group composition and makes requests to birth, merge, or disband a small group.
- Schedules and coordinates special outings for the group. Ensures that permissions are completed before each small group outside activity.
- Attends monthly student ministry team member meetings and updates team on ministry activities and action items.
- Performs other tasks as assigned or needed to ensure an effective ministry.

Knowledge, Skills, Abilities, and Other Characteristics
- Teaching and facilitation skills to lead a small group discussion.
- Knowledge of Scripture and/or ability to research a variety of topics to respond to questions, impart knowledge, and apply biblical principles to everyday situations facing teenagers and young adults.
- Leadership skills to guide a small group toward spiritual development.
- Knowledge of learning principles and techniques to apply a variety of approaches to teaching students sixth grade through college age, as assigned.
- Oral communication and active listening skills.
- Computer skills to send and receive e-mail and update attendance spreadsheets.

Special Qualifications
Impact Cell Group leaders must have a passion for Christ and a heart for seeing our teenagers live a life that is pleasing to Christ.

Special Physical Qualifications
None.

SERVICE DESCRIPTION
SMALL GROUP MINISTRY DIRECTOR

This file can also be found on the CD-ROM:

Part 2 > 3_The People > Service Descriptions > Small Group Ministry Director.doc

Ministry	Youth, Small Groups
Reports To	Youth Pastor
Duration of Ministry Opportunity	Ongoing

The desire of the student ministry is to have a spiritually grounded, focused, and life-changing ministry that glorifies God. The small group ministry director organizes and oversees the full operations and strategic planning process in consultation with the youth pastor.

Responsibilities

- Serves as ministry liaison with the Each One-Reach One Ministry, ensuring that the small group ministry aligns with the overall vision of small groups.
- Represents the ministry to external individuals or groups and provides training and information.
- Recommends establishing or disbanding of a small group.
- Approves all official announcements and correspondence related to small groups.
- Prepares a column for inclusion in the monthly newsletter to keep the congregation updated on ministry activities. Article must be submitted no later than the 15th of the month to ensure publication in the upcoming newsletter.
- Monitors small groups to assess performance and interaction between the facilitator and students.
- Surveys and follows up with small group leaders and students.
- Assists in providing training and resources to small group leaders to enhance their facilitation skills, group dynamics, and so on.
- Maintains all records and reports out to the pastor as requested.
- Researches and recommends small group curriculum.
- Participates in internal and external training and development.
- Attends monthly student ministry team member meetings and updates team on ministry activities and action items.
- Performs other tasks as assigned to ensure an effective ministry.

Knowledge, Skills, Abilities, and Other Characteristics
- Excellent coaching, leadership, and communication skills.
- Knowledge of Microsoft Word and Excel to prepare correspondence and reports; the Internet to send and receive e-mail; and the World Wide Web to research information.

Special Qualifications

The small group ministry director must have a passion for Christ and a heart for God's people. He/she must be able to oversee a relatively large ministry and design and implement strategies that integrate the desires and needs of the youth pastor, leaders, and students.

Special Physical Qualifications

None.

This file can also be found on the CD-ROM:

Part 2 > 3_The People > Service Descriptions > Membership Facilitator.doc

Ministry	Youth, Discipleship Ministry, Membership
Reports To	Youth Pastor
Duration of Ministry Opportunity	Ongoing

The desire of the student ministry is to have a spiritually grounded, focused, and life-changing ministry that glorifies God. The discipleship ministry is responsible for ensuring that teenagers and young adults choosing to follow Christ, rededicating their life, or accepting the call for membership during altar calls are appropriately assimilated into the church. The membership facilitator serves under the umbrella of the discipleship ministry and conducts membership classes and submits information for water baptisms to the baptism ministry for teenagers and young adults desiring to be baptized.

Responsibilities
- Develops and/or uses established curriculum to facilitate an interactive membership class for teenagers sixth grade through 18 years old.
- Completes and presents membership certificates.
- Provides the students' full name and the month the membership class or baptism was completed to the student ministry administrator for inclusion in the monthly student newsletter. This information must be provided no later than the 15th of each month to ensure publication in the upcoming month.
- Ensures a backup is available to conduct the membership class in case of a planned or emergency absence.
- Provides the student's name, telephone number, and parent's name to the baptism ministry leader for anyone desiring to be baptized. Completion of membership class is required for baptism.
- Follows up with teenagers (sixth grade through 18 years old) who have been baptized and schedules them for the membership class. Occasionally the Peace Baptist Church membership ministry will notify the teen ministry of a teenager being baptized without completing the membership class.

- Attends monthly student ministry team member meetings and updates team on ministry activities and action items.
- Prepares reports (such as number completed membership class, number of baptisms) upon request.
- Performs other tasks as assigned or needed to ensure an effective ministry.

Knowledge, Skills, Abilities, and Other Characteristics
- Knowledge of the "Romans Roadmap to Salvation" or similar outline to teach on salvation.
- Knowledge of the "Sinner's Prayer" to pray with the students during class.
- Strong organizational skills to carry out program requirements, follow up with students, and transfer information to the baptism ministry and the Peace Baptist Church membership ministry, upon request.
- Strong communications (verbal and listening) skills to facilitate and present a membership class.
- A thorough knowledge of the *ABC's of Christianity* and other foundational knowledge to present a membership class to teenagers (sixth grade through 18 years old).
- Basic knowledge of Microsoft Word and/or Excel to prepare correspondence and develop and/or maintain lists. Basic knowledge of e-mail to send and receive information.

Special Qualifications
Individuals who serve as a membership facilitator must have a passion for Christ, a heart to serve, and a discerning spirit to minister to individual and group needs.

Special Physical Qualifications
None.

SERVICE DESCRIPTION
MENTOR MINISTRY DIRECTOR

This file can also be found on the CD-ROM:

Part 2 > 3_The People > Service Descriptions > Mentor Ministry Director.doc

Ministry	Youth, Mentor Ministry
Reports To	Youth Pastor
Duration of Ministry Opportunity	Ongoing

The desire of the student ministry is to have a spiritually grounded, focused, and life-changing ministry that glorifies God. The mentor ministry director, in consultation with the youth pastor and collaboration with the women's ministry and men's ministry, organizes and oversees the full operations and strategies for an effective mentor ministry

Responsibilities
- In collaboration with others, defines the ministry vision, mission, goals, objectives, and scope. Serves as ministry liaison with the women's ministry and men's ministry, ensuring that the mentor ministry aligns with the overall vision, goals, and objectives of the church.
- Designs the organizational, program, and administrative structures, policies, and procedures of the ministry to ensure goals and objectives are achieved.
- Manages and delegates appropriate responsibilities to program team members.
- Represents the ministry to external individuals or groups and evaluates collaboration opportunities.
- Collaborates with the volunteer coordinator to recruit, screen, and assign ministry leadership.
- Evaluates program operations at least twice per year and conducts ongoing program assessments.
- Personally or through staff support, ensures that mentors and mentees are recruited, trained, screened, and appropriately matched, and provides follow-up support for mentor-mentee relationships.
- Personally, or through staff support, plans life-skills workshops, including identifying facilitators, curriculum, scope, and other necessary information.
- Approves all official announcements, correspondence, Web content, and other communication related to the mentor program.

- Prepares a column for inclusion in the monthly newsletter to keep the congregation updated on ministry activities. An article must be provided at least once a quarter and must be submitted no later than the 15th of the month to ensure publication in the upcoming newsletter.
- Trains and/or assists in providing training and resources to mentors to enhance mentor-mentee relationships.
- Maintains all records and reports out to the pastor as requested.
- Participates in internal and external training and development.
- Attends monthly student ministry team member meetings and updates team on ministry activities and action items.
- Performs other tasks as assigned to ensure an effective ministry.

Knowledge, Skills, Abilities, and Other Characteristics

- Knowledge of best practices in the mentoring field.
- Knowledge of general principles of volunteerism.
- Excellent coaching, leadership, and communication skills.
- Knowledge of Microsoft Word and Excel to prepare correspondence and reports; the Internet to send and receive e-mail; and the World Wide Web to research information.

Special Qualifications

The mentor ministry director must have a passion for Christ and a heart for God's people. He/she must be able to oversee a relatively large ministry and design and implement strategies that integrate the desires and needs of the youth pastor, mentors, and mentees.

Special Physical Qualifications

None.

SERVICE DESCRIPTION
MINISTRY-IN-MOTION COORDINATOR

This file can also be found on the CD-ROM:

Part 2 > 3_The People > Service Descriptions > Ministry-In-Motion Coordinator.doc

Ministry	Youth, Performing Arts
Reports To	Youth Pastor
Duration of Ministry Opportunity	Ongoing

The desire of the student ministry is to have a spiritually grounded, focused, and life-changing ministry that glorifies God. The Ministry-in-Motion coordinator ensures that the talent presented to the congregation glories God.

Responsibilities
- Recruits and auditions teenagers and young adults desiring to present their gift of rap, singing, step, dancing, and other skills and talents to the congregation.
- Schedules, follows up with, and confirms individuals and groups to minister through Ministry-in-Motion.
- Solicits and encourages teenagers and young adults to share their gifts through Ministry-in-Motion.
- Provides constructive feedback to teenagers and young adults desiring to share their gifts through Ministry-in-Motion.
- Recruits adults to minister through Ministry-in-Motion.
- Attends monthly student ministry team member meetings and updates team on ministry activities and action items, upon request.
- Performs other tasks as assigned or needed to ensure an effective ministry.

Knowledge, Skills, Abilities, and Other Characteristics
- Creativity and initiative to organize, manage, and oversee ministry activities.
- Computer skills to send and receive e-mails.
- Interpersonal skills to encourage high standards of spiritual commitment and excellence in participants.

Special Qualifications
The Ministry-in-Motion coordinator must have a passion for Christ, a heart to serve, and an understanding of the relationship to and impact of the arts on worship.

Special Physical Qualifications
None.

This file can also be found on the CD-ROM:

Part 2 > 3_The People > Service Descriptions > Performing Arts Coordinator.doc

Ministry	Youth, Performing Arts
Reports To	Youth Pastor
Duration of Ministry Opportunity	Ongoing

The desire of the student ministry is to have a spiritually grounded, focused, and life-changing ministry that glorifies God. The performing arts coordinator is responsible for creating and implementing the performing arts ministry and ensuring that the various teen arts ministries are coordinated and aligned with the overall vision of the youth pastor and the Peace Baptist Church worship and arts ministry.

Responsibilities
- Serves as the student ministry representative on the Peace Baptist Church Performing Arts Council. The Council meets monthly to plan the integration of the arts into the overall church ministry.
- Communicates with the teen drama ministry leader, choir director and praise team leader, and Ministry-in-Motion ministry coordinator on upcoming activities and the responsibilities of these respective ministry leaders.
- Consults with the youth pastor and ministry leaders on specific needs concerning the arts to determine the focus and creative approach.
- Submits ministry event requests to the PBC performing arts director to ensure the teen ministry needs are known. Follows up on requests and negotiates as needed.
- Ensures the drama ministry leader, choir director and praise team leader, and Ministry-in-Motion coordinator collaborate and coordinate on special events concerning the arts.
- Serves as the backup to the drama ministry leader upon request.
- Attends meetings required to plan for special events.
- Requests and solicits assistance and volunteers to assist with special events as needed.

- Attends monthly student ministry team member meetings and updates team on ministry activities and action items.
- Performs other tasks as assigned or needed to ensure an effective ministry.

Knowledge, Skills, Abilities, and Other Characteristics
- Creativity and initiative to organize, manage, and oversee ministry activities.
- Computer skills to send and receive e-mails.
- Interpersonal skills to encourage high standards of spiritual commitment and excellence in participants.

Special Qualifications
The performing arts coordinator must have a passion for Christ, a heart to serve, an intimate understanding of the relationship to and impact of the arts on worship, initiative, and the ability to strategically plan for and respond to ministry needs.

Special Physical Qualifications
None.

SERVICE DESCRIPTION
SERVICE COORDINATOR

This file can also be found on the CD-ROM:

Part 2 > 3_The People > Service Descriptions > Service Coordinator.doc

Ministry	Youth
Reports To	Youth Pastor
Duration of Ministry Opportunity	Ongoing

The desire of the student ministry is to have a spiritually grounded, focused, and life-changing ministry that glorifies God. The service coordinator has overall responsibility for ensuring that Sunday morning services are properly set up and executed effectively.

Responsibilities
- Connects laptop to projector to display weekly announcements.
- Shuts down laptop and returns to youth pastor.
- Ensures that a hard copy of the weekly announcements, provided by the administrative assistant, is placed in the pulpit.
- Ensures sanctuary is presentable upon opening and closing and all equipment is properly stored.
- Consults with the youth pastor on service requirements before and during service (such as dramas, Ministry in Motion, music and lighting requirements). Must be cognizant of all service activities for the assigned Sunday.
- Serves as support to other leaders as needed. May need to assume specific duties in the absence of an adult leader.
- Ensures that any last-minute instructions are relayed to the adult and teen volunteers.
- Secures a backup service coordinator in case of a planned or emergency absence.
- Performs other tasks as assigned or needed to ensure an effective ministry.

Knowledge, Skills, Abilities, and Other Characteristics
- Creativity and initiate to organize, manage, and oversee assigned Sunday morning service.

- Knowledge of overall flow of Sunday morning service to ensure service is executed efficiently.
- Ability to take initiative in preventing and/or correcting mishaps that may occur during service.
- Knowledge of special needs or instructions noted by the pastor.
- Basic knowledge of equipment connectivity.
- Computer skills to send and receive e-mail.

Special Qualifications
Individuals who serve as a service coordinator must have a passion for Christ, a heart to serve, and initiative to ensure Sunday morning service is executed efficiently.

Special Physical Qualifications
None.

SERVICE DESCRIPTION
SERVICE MUSICIAN

This file can also be found on the CD-ROM:

Part 2 > 3_The People > Service Descriptions > Service Musician.doc

Ministry	Youth, Praise and Worship
Reports To	Youth Pastor, Choir Director and Praise Team Leader
Duration of Ministry Opportunity	Ongoing

The desire of the student ministry is to have a spiritually grounded, focused, and life-changing ministry that glorifies God. The service musician is responsible for providing musical solos or accompaniment to the choir and/or praise team in the Sunday morning service and special events or as agreed by the choir director/praise team leader.

Responsibilities
- Attends choir/praise team rehearsals prepared to rehearse.
- Arrives at least 30 minutes before service starts to prepare for service.
- Provides music up to 10 minutes after benediction (closing of service).
- Consults with the choir director/praise team leader on ministry needs.
- Performs other tasks as assigned or needed to ensure an effective ministry.

Knowledge, Skills, Abilities, and Other Characteristics
- Gifted and talented in selected instrument (keyboard, drums, guitar, and so on).
- Ability to read music and/or "play by ear."

Special Qualifications
The service musician must have a passion for Christ, a heart to serve, an intimate understanding of the relationship to and impact of music on worship, and initiative to ensure the music ministry is executed with excellence.

Special Physical Qualifications
Ability to lift up to 20 pounds.

SERVICE DESCRIPTION
SOUND TECHNICIAN

This file can also be found on the CD-ROM:

Part 2 > 3_The People > Service Descriptions > Sound Technician.doc

Ministry	Youth, Sound and Lighting
Reports To	Youth Pastor
Duration of Ministry Opportunity	Ongoing

The desire of the student ministry is to have a spiritually grounded, focused, and life-changing ministry that glorifies God. The sound technician assembles, operates, and maintains technical equipment to amplify, enhance, record, mix, or reproduce sound for Sunday morning service and special events.

Responsibilities
- Sets up, tests, and operates equipment to optimize sound quality and eliminate sound distortions.
- Selects, places, and adjusts microphones.
- Monitors audio signals to detect quality deviations or malfunctions.
- Records messages, music, and other sounds on tapes and/or CDs.
- Reproduces and duplicates sound recordings from original recording media using sound editing and duplication equipment.
- Troubleshoots and solves technical problems.
- Keeps logs of recordings.
- Consults with the youth pastor on system needs, expenditures, equipment problems, and other details. Ensures that required repairs are made.
- Attends monthly student ministry team member meetings and updates team on ministry activities and action items, upon request.
- Trains others on the use of equipment.
- Performs other tasks as assigned or needed to ensure an effective ministry.

Knowledge, Skills, Abilities, and Other Characteristics
- Creativity and initiative to organize, manage, and oversee ministry activities.
- Technical knowledge of sound equipment to optimize sound quality and make recordings.
- Knowledge of the World Wide Web to research related information.
- Computer skills to send and receive e-mails.

Special Qualifications
The sound technician must have a passion for Christ, a heart to serve, an intimate understanding of the relationship to and impact of music on worship, and initiative to ensure the ministry is executed with excellence.

Special Physical Qualifications
Ability to lift up to 50 pounds.

This file can also be found on the CD-ROM:

Part 2 > 3_The People > Service Descriptions > Special Events Coordinator.doc

Ministry	Youth, Special Events
Reports To	Youth Pastor
Duration of Ministry Opportunity	Ongoing

The desire of the student ministry is to have a spiritually grounded, focused, and life-changing ministry that glorifies God. The special events coordinator plans one-time and annual special events for the teenagers and young adults that will foster fellowship and spiritual growth.

Responsibilities
- Identifies one-time and annual special events for the teenagers and young adults that will foster fellowship and spiritual growth. Events may occur outside or inside the church. Presents suggestions to the youth pastor for approval.
- Develops 3-month, 6-month, and 12-month calendars to ensure adequate preparation and notification of special events.
- Researches related information (such as cost, accommodations, transportation) for all special events and presents a budget to the youth pastor for approval at least 60 days in advance of the event.
- Drafts fliers, posters, postcards, and announcements for placement in the bulletin or The Messenger to promote the special event and coordinates with the student ministry administrator for final design and printing. Posts fliers and places announcements in conspicuous areas to ensure the greatest exposure.
- Sets up exhibits and sign-up tables to ensure that teenagers and parents know the scope and requirements of the special event (such as dates, times, locations, accommodations, transportation, cost), collects payments and permission slips, answers questions, and offers any other assistance necessary.
- Develops checklists to ensure special events are adequately planned.
- Provides instructions to and coordinates with the ministry leaders for the ushers and greeters and/or Visitors Welcome Desk to hand out announcements for special events before and/or after service as appropriate.

- Requests and solicits assistance and volunteers to assist with special events as needed.
- Attends monthly student ministry team member meetings and updates team on ministry activities and action items.
- Performs other tasks as assigned or needed to ensure an effective ministry.

Knowledge, Skills, Abilities, and Other Characteristics
- Creativity and initiative to identify, organize, manage, and oversee ministry activities.
- Knowledge of the World Wide Web to research activities.
- Knowledge of special event planning to ensure events are adequately planned and executed.
- Computer skills to prepare correspondence and announcements and send and receive e-mails.
- Knowledge of basic budgeting to develop, monitor, and reconcile receipts and expenses.

Special Qualifications
The special events coordinator must have a passion for Christ, a heart to serve, and initiative to ensure special events for the teenagers/young adults are well coordinated.

Special Physical Qualifications
None.

SERVICE DESCRIPTION
SPECIAL EVENTS TEAM MEMBER

This file can also be found on the CD-ROM:

Part 2 > 3_The People > Service Descriptions > Special Events Team Member.doc

Ministry	Youth, Special Events
Reports To	Youth Pastor, Special Events Coordinator
Duration of Ministry Opportunity	Ongoing

The desire of the student ministry is to have a spiritually grounded, focused, and life-changing ministry that glorifies God. The special events team member assists with planning one-time and annual special events for the teenagers and young adults that will foster fellowship and spiritual growth.

Responsibilities

- Identifies one-time and annual special events for the teenagers and young adults that will foster fellowship and spiritual growth. Events may occur outside or inside the church. Presents suggestions to special events coordinator.
- Researches related information (such as cost, accommodations, transportation) for all special events and presents findings to special events coordinator.
- Assists coordinator with drafting fliers, posters, postcards, and announcements for placement in the bulletin or The Messenger to promote the special event. Posts fliers and places announcements in conspicuous areas to ensure the greatest exposure.
- Sets up exhibits and sign-up tables to ensure that teenagers and parents know the scope and requirements of the special event (such as dates, times, locations, accommodations, transportation, cost), collects payments and permission slips, answers questions, and offers any other assistance necessary.
- Provides information to with the ministry leaders for the ushers and greeters and/or Visitors Welcome Desk to hand out announcements for special events before and/or after service as appropriate.
- Attends monthly student ministry team member meetings and updates team on ministry activities and action items.
- Phones and e-mails parents and teenagers to ensure students are kept abreast of payment schedules and deadline dates.
- Performs other tasks as assigned or needed to ensure an effective ministry.

Knowledge, Skills, Abilities, and Other Characteristics
- Knowledge of the World Wide Web to research activities.
- Knowledge of special event planning to assist with ensuring events are adequately planned and executed.
- Computer skills to prepare correspondence and announcements and send and receive e-mails.

Special Qualifications

Individuals serving on the special events team must have a passion for Christ, a heart to serve, and initiative to ensure special events for the teenagers/young adults are well coordinated.

Special Physical Qualifications

None.

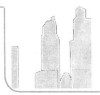

SERVICE DESCRIPTION
TEEN DRAMA COORDINATOR

This file can also be found on the CD-ROM:

Part 2 > 3_The People > Service Descriptions > Teen Drama Coordinator.doc

Ministry	Youth, Performing Arts
Reports To	Youth Pastor
Duration of Ministry Opportunity	Ongoing

The desire of the student ministry is to have a spiritually grounded, focused, and life-changing ministry that glorifies God. The teen drama coordinator coordinates ministry activities and ensures that the various plays, skits, and monologues presented by the student ministry are consistent with the vision of the youth pastor and the church overall.

Responsibilities

- Serves as a drama coach for novice and experienced teen actors and actresses.
- Consults with the youth pastor and ministry leaders on specific needs concerning plays, skits, illustrative messages, monologues, or other presentations.
- Identifies off-the-shelf scripts and/or writes scripts for presentation to the student ministry congregation and as an outreach vehicle for the student ministry.
- Assists with directing plays, skits, and illustrative messages.
- Recruits teenagers to serve in the drama ministry including actors/actresses, props personnel, writers, directors, sound and lighting technicians, makeup artists, ushers/greeters, marketing, and hospitality. Notifies the teen volunteer coordinator of ministry needs.
- Establishes and enforces guidelines for the drama ministry.
- Schedules, coordinates, and oversees rehearsals.
- Advertises for auditions and open calls. Sends announcements to the service administrator to ensure the announcement is part of the Sunday morning announcements.
- Submits requests to the teen performing arts coordinator for adults to participate in a play, a skit, or a monologue presented by the student ministry. Requests are forwarded to the PBC performing arts director for action.
- Purchases and/or prepares requisitions for ministry supplies.
- Maintains, monitors, and reconciles the teen drama ministry budget.

- Attends meetings required to plan for special events.
- Requests and solicits assistance and volunteers to assist with special events as needed.
- Attends monthly student ministry team member meetings and updates team on ministry activities and action items.
- Performs other tasks as assigned or needed to ensure an effective ministry.

Knowledge, Skills, Abilities, and Other Characteristics
- Overall knowledge of the arts and acting techniques, and requirements for a full or partial production.
- Creativity and initiative to organize, manage, and oversee ministry activities.
- Computer skills to send and receive e-mails.
- Interpersonal skills to encourage high standards of spiritual commitment and excellence in participants.

Special Qualifications
The performing arts coordinator must have a passion for Christ, a heart to serve, an intimate understanding of the relationship to and impact of the arts on worship, initiative, and the ability to strategically plan for and respond to ministry needs.

Special Physical Qualifications
None.

SERVICE DESCRIPTION

VISITORS AND WELCOME DESK MINISTRY LEADER

This file can also be found on the CD-ROM:

Part 2 > 3_The People > Service Descriptions > Visitors and Welcome Desk Ministry Leader.doc

Ministry	Youth, Visitors and Welcome Desk
Reports To	Youth Pastor
Duration of Ministry Opportunity	Ongoing

The desire of the student ministry is to have a spiritually grounded, focused, and life-changing ministry that glorifies God. The Visitors and Welcome Desk Team works closely with the Greeters and Ushers Ministry to ensure that members and visitors feel welcome during Sunday morning service and special events.

Responsibilities

- Oversees the Visitors and Welcome Desk, ensuring that visitor cards are collected for each visitor and that each visitor is acknowledged with follow-up correspondence.
- Sets up the Visitors and Welcome Desk 20 minutes before Sunday morning service begins, during special events, and when requested. Setup includes, at a minimum, placement of tablecloth, visitor cards and clipboards, brochures, newsletters, sign-up sheets, pens, and any other information related to the student ministry (such as surveys).
- Maintains a stock of visitor cards, follow-up visitor cards, pens, brochures, sign-up sheets, and other materials as needed.
- Ensures that visitor cards, brochures, newsletters, and sign-up sheets are readily available. Coordinates with and submits requests to the church's communications administrator to print visitor cards and follow-up visitor cards. Notifies the student ministry administrator when brochures, newsletters, and sign-up sheets are needed. Requests must be submitted at least one week in advance to ensure availability.
- Coordinates with the teen greeters and ushers ministry to administer and collect visitor cards.
- Sends visitors follow-up postcards within 48 hours of their visit. Ensures that stamps for mailing correspondence are available. Contacts the youth pastor or submits a purchase order or request for reimbursement.

- Collects sign-up sheets and forwards to the respective ministry leader at the end of each service.
- Provides training and direction to teenagers and adults manning the Visitors and Welcome Desk.
- Stores materials for the Visitors and Welcome Desk in a safe place at the end of service or special event.
- Forwards visitor cards (after mailing follow-up visitor card) to the respective ministry (such as Prayer or HOPE) to ensure that the visitor's needs are addressed.
- Ensures that candy bags/cups are available for first-time teen/young adult visitors to the student ministry.
- Hands out candy bags/cups upon receipt of the visitor card.
- Prepares visitor reports upon request.
- Attends monthly student ministry team member meetings and updates team on ministry activities and action items.
- Performs other tasks as assigned or needed to ensure an effective ministry.

Knowledge, Skills, Abilities, and Other Characteristics
- Creativity and initiative to organize, manage, and oversee a ministry.
- Overall knowledge of Peace Baptist Church ministries and facilities to provide information and/or direct visitors to the appropriate location or ministry contact person.
- Initiative to address visitors' needs.
- Strong organizational skills to manage program requirements, follow up with visitors, and receive and transfer information to respective ministries.
- Computer skills to send and receive e-mail.

Special Qualifications
The individual who oversees the Visitors and Welcome Desk must have a passion for Christ, a heart to serve, a welcoming spirit, and initiative to ensure our visitors' needs are addressed.

Special Physical Qualifications
Ability to lift up to 15 pounds.

This file can also be found on the CD-ROM:

Part 2 > 3_The People > Service Descriptions > Visitors and Welcome Desk Ministry Team Member.doc

Ministry	Youth, Visitors and Welcome Desk
Reports To	Youth Pastor
Duration of Ministry Opportunity	Ongoing

The desire of the student ministry is to have a spiritually grounded, focused, and life-changing ministry that glorifies God. The Visitors and Welcome Desk Team works closely with the Greeters and Ushers Ministry to ensure that members and visitors feel welcome during Sunday morning service and special events.

Responsibilities

- Sets up the Visitors and Welcome Desk 20 minutes before Sunday morning service begins, during special events, and when requested. Setup includes, at a minimum, placement of tablecloth, visitor cards and clipboards, brochures, newsletters, sign-up sheets, pens, and any other information related to the student ministry (such as surveys).
- Coordinates with the teen greeters and ushers ministry to administer and collect visitor cards.
- Sends visitors follow-up postcards within 48 hours of their visit.
- Collects sign-up sheets and forwards to the respective ministry leader at the end of each service.
- Stores materials for the Visitors and Welcome Desk in a safe place at the end of service or special event.
- Ensures that candy bags/cups are available for first-time teen/young adult visitors to the student ministry.
- Hands out candy bags/cups upon receipt of the visitor card.
- Prepares visitor reports upon request.
- Performs other tasks as assigned or needed to ensure an effective ministry.

Knowledge, Skills, Abilities, and Other Characteristics

- Overall knowledge of Peace Baptist Church ministries and facilities to provide information and/or direct visitors to the appropriate location or ministry contact person.
- Initiative to address visitors' needs.
- Computer skills to send and receive e-mail.

Special Qualifications

The individual who serves on the Visitors and Welcome Desk Team must have a passion for Christ, a heart to serve, a welcoming spirit, and initiative to ensure our visitors' needs are addressed.

Special Physical Qualifications

Ability to lift up to 15 pounds.

SERVICE DESCRIPTION
VOLUNTEER COORDINATOR (ADULTS)

This file can also be found on the CD-ROM:

Part 2 > 3_The People > Service Descriptions > Volunteer Coordinator.doc

Ministry	Youth
Reports To	Youth Pastor
Duration of Ministry Opportunity	Ongoing

The desire of the student ministry is to have a spiritually grounded, focused, and life-changing ministry that glorifies God. The volunteer coordinator oversees the recruitment, screening, and assimilation of volunteer adult leaders and team members.

Responsibilities

- Identifies volunteer ministry needs and opportunities based on actual or planned ministries and programs.
- Consults with ministry leaders concerning volunteer opportunities in their respective ministries and receives requests from adult leaders.
- Plans recruitment activities including announcements, Meet-and-Greet, informational sessions, and other promotional methods.
- Presents the student ministry at membership meetings, Ministry Walks, and during special events.
- Interviews and responds via telephone, e-mail, or personal conversation to people desiring to serve in the student ministry.
- Ensures volunteers complete information for background check. Submits information to the student ministry administrator for action.
- Plans and schedules New Volunteer Orientation/Heart of the Youth Pastor for individuals electing to serve in the student ministry.
- Plans and schedules volunteer appreciation events.
- Collaborates with the adult leader in writing a service description for each volunteer opportunity.
- Follows up with volunteers and ministry leaders 30, 60, and 90 days from their initial service to ensure mutual needs are being met.
- Sends "Thank You" cards to volunteers who completed the orientation.

- Ensures orientation handbook and service descriptions are updated and available to new and prospective volunteers.
- Develops and maintains appropriate record/retrieval systems for needs, interests, and skills of members.
- Serves as the student ministry representative for the Peace Baptist Church Volunteer Ministry ensuring that ministry needs are represented and integrated into the overall vision of the church.
- Attends monthly student ministry team member meetings and updates team on ministry activities and action items.
- Performs other tasks as assigned to ensure an effective ministry.

Knowledge, Skills, Abilities, and Other Characteristics
- Overall knowledge of the student ministry to identify volunteer needs.
- Creativity and initiative to organize, manage, and oversee a ministry.
- Knowledge of general principles of volunteerism.
- Strong organizational skills to manage program requirements, follow up with volunteers, and transfer information to the respective ministry.
- Strong interpersonal skills to recruit and retain volunteers.
- Computer skills to prepare correspondence, send and receive e-mail, and maintain database.
- Strong communication skills to present the student ministry as an excellent ministry to serve.

Special Qualifications
The individual who serves as the adult leader volunteer must have a passion for Christ, a heart to serve, and comfort interacting with individuals and representing the needs and desires of the student ministry.

Special Physical Qualifications
None.

VISITOR INFORMATION

This sample form is a simple first step in getting to know the students who visit your youth ministry. If possible, use this same type of content on a postcard-sized piece of cardstock with your ministry or church logo on it to give a more appealing look.

This file can also be found on the CD-ROM:
Part 2 > 4_The Programs > Sample Visitor Information Card.pdf

Side 1

Visitor's Information

Thank you for visiting Student Impact @ Peace Baptist Church.
Please complete both sides of the visitors card and turn it in at the front desk for your gift.

Name   Date of Birth

Mailing Address

City   State   Zip Code

Home Telephone Number   Cell or Other Telephone Number

E-mail Address

Name of School

Grade or Class

Are you member of a church? [ ]Yes [ ]No If yes, which church? _____
Do you want someone to contact you regarding salvation/accepting Christ as your Savior? [ ]Yes [ ]No

Tell Us About Yourself

What's Your Favorite...

Candy Bar _____

Color _____

Movie _____

Sport _____

Game _____

What do you like to do in your spare time? _____

How can we pray for you? _____

CENSUS FORM

This sample form is an efficient way for the families at your church to provide their information to the youth ministry. This info can provide you with contact information that can be used for marketing, emergency contacts, and providing a better understanding of the families at your church.

This file can also be found on the CD-ROM:
Part 2 > 4_The Programs > Sample Census Form.doc

PEACE BAPTIST CHURCH YOUTH DEPARTMENT
CENSUS FORM
Because you matter to us

Household Name:
(Parents/Guardians) _____

Address Line 1: _____

Address Line 2: _____

City: _____ State: _____ ZIP Code: _____

Home Phone: _____

Individual 1: (Student)

Last Name: _____ First Name: _____

Home Phone: _____ Cell Phone: _____

E-mail Address: _____

Date of Birth: _____ Grade: _____   Male   Female

School Attending: _____

Area of Interest in Ministry: _____

Member of Peace? Yes   No   Date Joined (month/yr): _____

Individual 2: Sisters or Brothers in Household (List Below)
(If you have more then one, list as many as possible on lines below)

Last Name: _____ First Name: _____

Home Phone: _____ Cell Phone: _____

E-mail Address: _____

Date of Birth: _____ Grade: _____   Male   Female

School Attending: _____

Area of Interest in Ministry: _____

Member of Peace? Yes   No   Date Joined (month/yr): _____

Other Siblings: _____

Individual 3: Child/Other (Circle One)

Last Name: _____ First Name: _____

Home Phone: _____ Cell Phone: _____

E-mail Address: _____

Date of Birth: _____ Grade: _____   Male   Female

Marital Status: _____ Anniversary Date: _____

Member of Peace? Yes   No   Date Joined (month/yr): _____

Individual 4: Child/Other (Circle One)

Last Name: _____ First Name: _____

Home Phone: _____ Cell Phone: _____

E-mail Address: _____

Date of Birth: _____ Grade: _____   Male   Female

Marital Status: _____   Anniversary Date: _____

Member of Peace?   Yes   No   Date Joined (month/yr): _____

Individual 5: Child/Other (Circle One)

Last Name: _____ First Name: _____

Home Phone: _____ Cell Phone: _____

E-mail Address: _____

Date of Birth: _____ Grade: _____   Male   Female

Marital Status: _____   Anniversary Date: _____

Member of Peace?   Yes   No   Date Joined (month/yr): _____

"Head of Household" may be male or female; "Spouse" may be male or female; "Children" includes children (in and outside of the home) who participate in Peace programs; "Other" includes immediate family members (such as grandparents, aunts, uncles) who live in household.

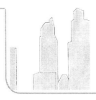

REGISTRATION PACKET

This sample registration packet can be modified for a variety events like recreation leagues, camps, retreats, and so on. Please make sure to check with your senior pastor for updated legal language that your church may prefer to use.

This file can also be found on the CD-ROM:
Part 2 > 4_The Programs > Sample Registration Packet.doc

PEACE SAINTS BASKETBALL PACKET

Welcome!

Hello, parents! We are excited to be starting a new basketball season at Peace Baptist. We're even more excited that you and your child are joining us! This is our second year of basketball, and we anticipate a good time and lots of learning for our children.
We expect our children to have fun, but we expect them to work hard as well! Thank you for joining us for our parent meeting. We will be giving you more information about the teams and season.

Please find enclosed in this package:
- Peace Baptist Church Personal Information Form
- Peace Baptist Church Liability and Photo Release
- Players' Rules & Regulations

The registration fee for this season is $100. There will be fundraisers during the season to help offset additional league fees. Each team member will be expected to participate.

NO PLAYER WILL BE ABLE TO PRACTICE, PLAY, OR RECEIVE A UNIFORM WITHOUT PAYING FEES AND HAVING ALL INFORMATION TURNED IN!!!

If you have any questions please feel free to contact Pastor Jeff. Thank you in advance for all of your support and dedication.

Sincerely,
Pastor Jeff

PERSONAL INFORMATION FORM:

Player's Information

Name _____
      First   Last

Home Phone _____ **Cell Phone** _____

Address _____

City _____ **State** _____ **ZIP** _____

Birthday ____ / ____ / _____   **Grade** _____   **School** _____
          MM   DD   YYYY

Jersey Size _____ **Shorts Size** _____ **T-shirt Size** _____

Mother's Information

Name _____
      First   Last

Home Phone _____ **Cell Phone** _____

Address _____

City _____ **State** _____ **ZIP** _____

Father's Information

Name _____
      First   Last

Home Phone _____ **Cell Phone** _____

Address _____

City _____ **State** _____ **ZIP** _____

Pick-Up Information

Custodial Parent _____ Mother _____ Father _____ Both

Can either parent pick up child?   Yes   No

Other people who can pick up:	Name	Phone Number

Insurance Information

Physician _____
       First   Last

Address _____

City _____ State _____ ZIP _____

Phone _____

Insurance _____ Policy # _____

Group ID _____ Phone _____

Allergies: _____

Medications: _____

LIABILITY RELEASE:

I, the undersigned parent or guardian, do hereby grant permission for my child, whose name is _____ and hereinafter shall be referred to as "participant," to participate in the Peace Saints Basketball Ministry conducted by Peace Baptist Church. I grant permission for said participant to receive the necessary medical treatment in the event of an injury or illness. I hereby hold Peace Baptist Church and its representatives and its subsidiaries now and future harmless in the exercise of this authority. I further acknowledge, understand, and agree that in taking part in this program, there is possibility of risk of injury or illness and that participant is assuming the risk of such illness or injury by participation. I further agree to hold harmless Peace Baptist Church, including, but not limited to, rehearsals, social activities, practices, competitions, and/or other activity associated with the course of the athletic year, including travel to and from such activities.

I hereby waive and absolve Peace Baptist Church and all divisions of personnel and subsidiaries thereof any liability and responsibility of injuries, sickness, accidents, and/ or acts of God incurred during participation in clinics, private coaching, practices, performances, choreography, competitions, and/or other related ability by my child, _____ . In consideration of my signed release allowing my child to participate in the Peace Saints Basketball Ministry, I, intending to be legally bound do hereby, my heirs, executor and administration, waive, release, and forever discharge any and all rights and claims for damage which my child known as participant or I may have or which may hereafter accrue to me or my participant child against Peace Baptist Church or their staff, coaches, and subsidiaries for any participation in or out of travel to and/or return from respective Peace Baptist Church site, 1399 Austin Dr. Decatur, GA 30032.

Child's Name _____ Date _____

Parent's Name _____

Signature _____

PHOTO RELEASE:

I hereby grant permission to the Peace Baptist Church to use my child, _____'s, photograph on its World Wide Web site or in other official printed publication without further consideration, and I acknowledge the church's right to crop or treat the photograph at its discretion. I also acknowledge that the church may choose not to use my photo at this time, but may do so at its own discretion at a later date. I also understand that once my image is posted on Peace Baptist Church's website, the image can be downloaded by any other computer user. Therefore, I agree to indemnify and hold harmless from any claims to Peace Baptist Church and all divisions of personnel and subsidiaries.

Peace Baptist Church reserves the right to discontinue use of photos without notice.

Child's Name _____ Date _____

Parent's Name _____

Signature _____

PLAYER'S RULES & REGULATIONS:

- "Sagging" is not allowed; your underwear is not to be seen during practice or game time.
- Tardiness is not acceptable for either practices or games.
- Bad language and overly aggressive behavior will not be permitted at any time. Words such as the "N" word or fighting are grounds for suspension or getting kicked off the team.
- Cell phone usage during practice is prohibited.
- School Progress Reports will be monitored throughout the season.

I have read all of the rules and regulations above and hereby agree to them. I understand that if any of these rules are broken I am subject to consequences presented by the Coach.

Player's Signature _____ Date _____

Parent's Signature _____ Date _____

PARENTAL CONSENT AND MEDICAL RELEASE FORM

Many of the activities that youth ministries go on including camps or retreats, trips to ball games, amusement parks, and other locations carry a certain amount of risk. This form can help parents understand the inherent risks and potentially release the youth ministry and church from legal responsibility. While we've provided you with this sample, please check with your senior pastor to ensure that the legal language that your church is comfortable with is included.

This file can also be found on the CD-ROM:
Part 2 > 4_The Programs > Sample Parental Consent and Medical Release Form.doc

PARENTAL CONSENT AND MEDICAL RELEASE FORM

I,_____, am the parent or legal guardian of
_____ who was born on _____, year _____. I warrant that I posses all the rights, powers, and privileges of a parent or legal guardian necessary to execute this legal instrument with binding legal effect.

As a parent or legal guardian of _____, I certify and affirm that I have been completely and thoroughly informed that as a youth attending Peace Baptist Church, my child will participate in certain activities that carry with them a degree of risk and danger.

Examples of risky and dangerous activities include, but are not limited to:
1. physical activities, both indoors and outdoors;
2. sports, both informal and organized;
3. use of recreational equipment;
4. field trips, both on and off campus;
5. travel by automobile;
6. activities around water, including swimming and boating;
7. hiking; and camping.

I acknowledge and understand that _____ may offer other activities not listed above that present similar risks or dangers to my child.

I consent to my child's participation in these activities. I acknowledge and understand that this PARENTAL CERTIFICATION, CONSENT AND RELEASE has the same force and effect regardless of whether the activities engaged in are free or if a fee is charged.

Further, I personally assume, on my child's behalf, all risk in connection with said activities for any harm, injury, or damages that may befall my child as a result of my child's participation in the activities, whether foreseen or unforeseen, and I still wish to allow my child to proceed with the activities.

I acknowledge and agree that _____ shall not be held liable in any way for any occurrence resulting directly or indirectly from these activities that results in injury, death, or any other damages to my child, me, or my family, heirs, or assigns. In consideration of my child being allowed to participate in these activities, on behalf of my child, I hereby personally assume all risk in connection with said activities, for any harm, injury, or damage that may befall my child, me, or my family, heirs, or assigns while engaged in such activities.

I understand that the terms herein are contractual and not mere recital; I have signed this document as my own free act. It is my intentions by signing this document to exempt and release Peace Baptist Church from all liability whatsoever for personal injury, property damage, or wrongful death caused by negligence.

I further acknowledge and agree that my signature on this PARENTAL CERTIFICATION, CONSENT AND RELEASE shall constitute a bar to any recovery by my child, me, or my family, heirs, or assigns in all suits and actions that may be instituted against Peace Baptist Church, its agents, servants, or employees for injuries or death to my child, whether or not same resulted from the negligence of Peace Baptist Church, its agents, servants, or employees, or due to the negligence of my child, or due to the risks ordinarily incident to my child's participation in these activities, or due to the contributory negligence of my child.

I understand that it is my obligation to inform the management of Peace Baptist Church of any and all health considerations or medical conditions that would restrict my child's participation in any and all activities while at _____.

I have fully informed myself of the contents of this PARENTAL CERTIFICATION, CONSENT AND RELEASE by reading it before I signed it.

Date _____

_____
Signature

_____
Print name

MEDICAL RELEASE FORM

Student's Information

Name _____
      First   Last

Home Phone _____ **Cell Phone** _____

Address _____

City _____ **State** _____ **ZIP** _____

Birthday _____ / _____ / _____
            MM   DD   YYYY

Emergency Contact #1

Name _____
      First   Last

Home Phone _____ **Cell Phone** _____

Address _____

City _____ **State** _____ **ZIP** _____

Emergency Contact #2

Name _____
      First   Last

Home Phone _____ **Cell Phone** _____

Address _____

City _____ **State** _____ **ZIP** _____

Insurance Information

Physician _____
        First   Last

Address _____

City _____ State _____ ZIP _____

Phone _____

Insurance _____ Policy # _____

Group ID _____ Phone _____

Allergies: _____

Medications: _____

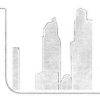

ACTIVITY PERMISSION SLIP

Keeping parents in the loop with the various activities of the youth ministry is crucial. That's why items like an activity permission slip can be an important tool when it comes to those events and activities that are considered out of the norm. Please make sure to check with your senior pastor in case your form needs additional release of liability.

This file can also be found on the CD-ROM:
Part 2 > 4_The Programs > Sample Activity Permission Slip.doc

ACTIVITY PERMISSION SLIP

I hereby give _____ my permission to participate with the youth ministry of Peace Baptist Church (NAME OF EVENT). I understand adults from Peace Baptist Church will provide transportation. My child and I are both aware that there are certain risks associated with any activity, and we accept those risks.

My child agrees to obey all the rules and regulations established by the leaders of this activity and the rules that are in place by Peace Baptist Church Youth Ministry leadership.

In the event of any emergency, I give my permission for leaders of this event to seek medical treatment for my child.

____ I will pick up my child at Peace Baptist Church by _____ p.m.
____ My child will be dropped off at home by _____ p.m.

_____
Signature of Parent or Guardian

_____
Home Phone   Cell Phone

_____
Alternate Emergency Contact (Name and Phone Number)

_____
Date

ALTAR CALL LETTER

As youth workers, our main goal is to point teenagers toward a life with Jesus. Recognizing that life-changing commitment is just the first step of many that needs to be taken in helping students along their faith journey. This sample altar call letter is a simple way to help celebrate the commitment, but also point a teenager toward the next steps in faith development.

This file can also be found on the CD-ROM:
Part 2 > 4_The Programs > Sample Altar Call Letter.doc

Dear John:

I want to take a moment to thank you for opening your heart and responding to the Lord's plans for your life this past Wednesday at Tha Brick House Unleashed II Youth Conference at Peace Baptist Church. It was truly an awesome evening.

I want to encourage you in your important decision to receive Jesus Christ as your Lord and Savior. As a brand-new "baby" Christian, you need to grow and mature in Christ. Here are the four things that will cause you to grow quickly:

1. Read and study the Word of God daily. (II Timothy 2:15)
2. Spend time in prayer, talking to God. (Hebrews 4:16)
3. Make a commitment to attend service Tha Brick House weekly. (Hebrews 10:25)
4. Share Christ with others you know who need him. (Mark 16:15)

Here is a great way to make all of those things happen at once. Go to the Youth Firm Foundation Discipleship Desk next Wednesday/Sunday located (location) and enroll in the Youth Firm Foundation Program. This is a special program that will develop you spiritually, as well as make you a member of Peace Baptist Church and a candidate for baptism. Upon completion of the program, you will be presented with a special certificate and gift from Pastor Barnette and myself on a Sunday during adult worship.

May God continue to bless and prosper you as you serve him with all your heart. It is a privilege to be your youth pastor.

Your friend in Christ,

Pastor Jeff

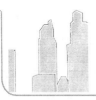

YOUTH MEMBERSHIP CLASS

Helping students understand what we believe as Christians and making them a part of a church family is a critical step in the faith development process. On the CD-ROM you'll find a sample PowerPoint presentation that you can adapt for the students at your church. We realize that each church may have a different way of approaching baptism, communion, and so on, so we encourage you to modify this presentation to match the needs of your church.

This file can be found on the CD-ROM:
Part 2 > 4_The Programs > Sample Youth Membership Class.ppt

ASSIMILATION PROCESS

Getting teenagers to show up to your midweek or weekend services is a great thing to have going for you. Getting them connected to other Christians and the church body as a whole is a little more difficult. It takes a well-defined and well-coordinated effort to make sure that students don't "fall through the cracks." This sample assimilation process can help you take care of the students that God has brought into your ministry, as well as help them move along their faith journey.

This file can also be found on the CD-ROM:
Part 2 > 4_The Programs > Sample Assimilation Process.doc

VISITOR FLOW CHART

1st Time Visitor

1 Visitor comes to church → **2** Welcome is given in service → **3** Visitor fills out visitor card

6 Visitor receives a follow-up phone call ← **5** Visitor is sent a visitor's postcard ← **4** Visitor info put into "the system"

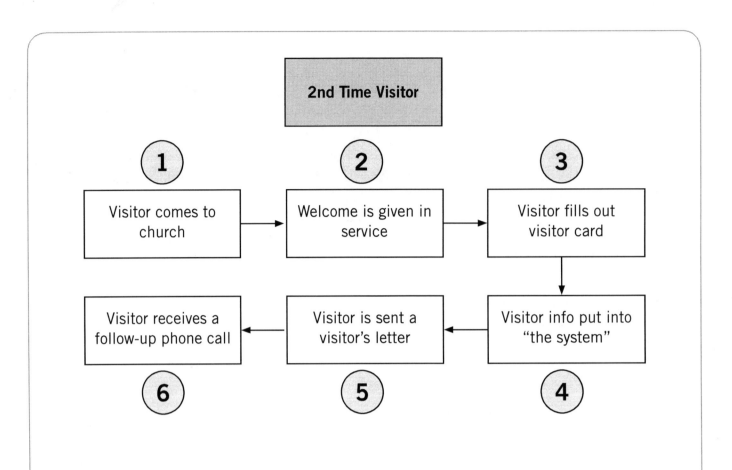

2nd Time Visitor

1. Visitor comes to church
2. Welcome is given in service
3. Visitor fills out visitor card
4. Visitor info put into "the system"
5. Visitor is sent a visitor's letter
6. Visitor receives a follow-up phone call

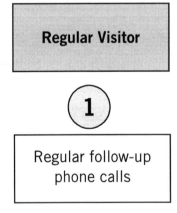

Regular Visitor

1. Regular follow-up phone calls

DISCIPLESHIP PROCESS

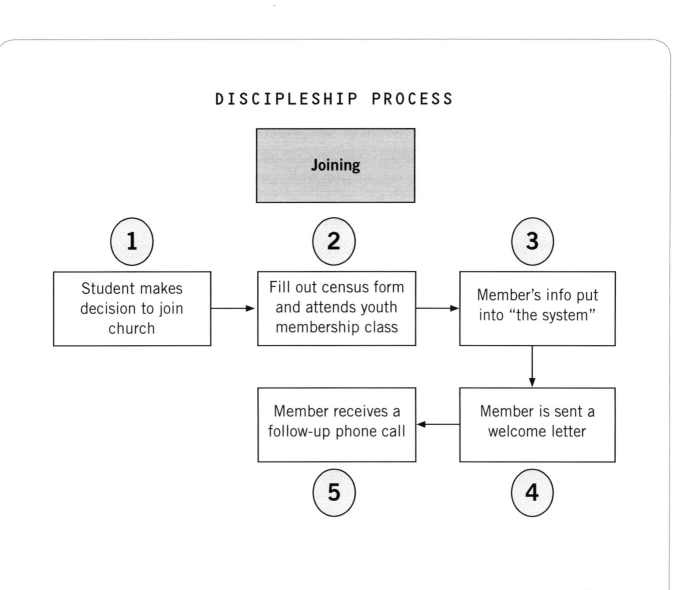

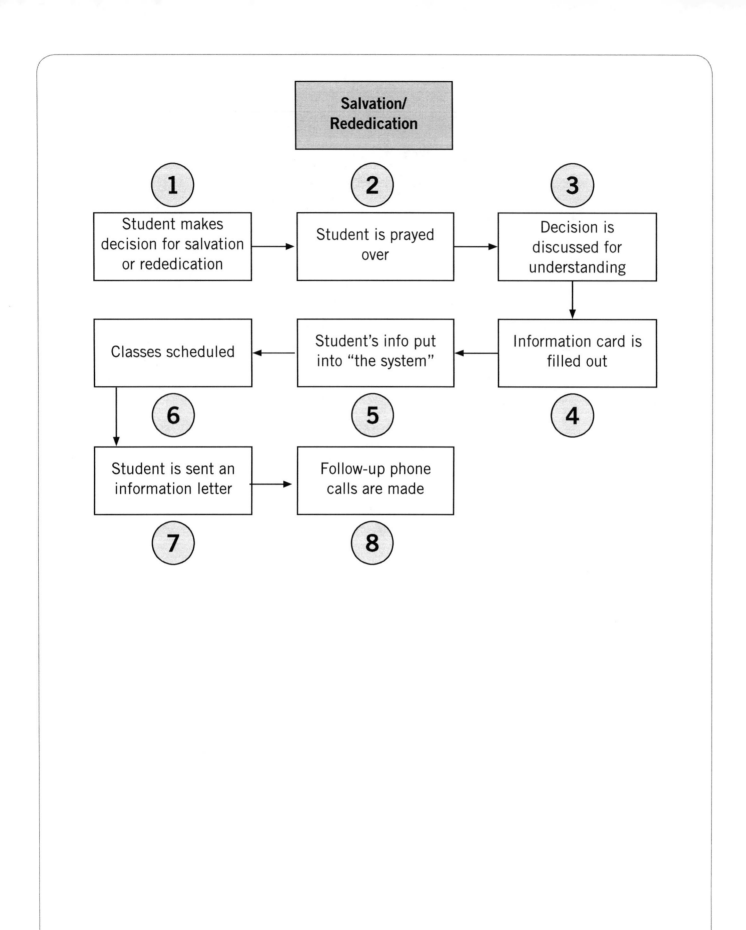

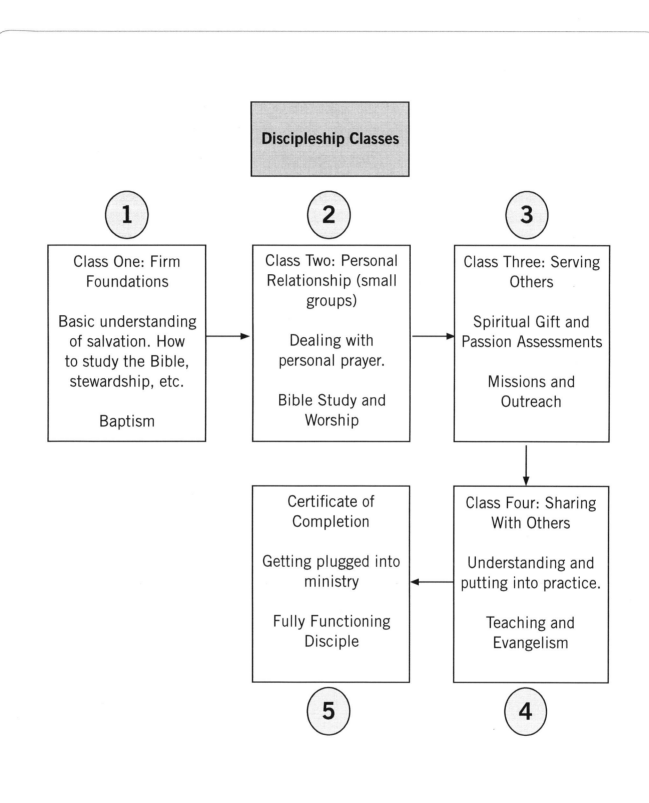

Discipleship Classes

1

Class One: Firm Foundations

Basic understanding of salvation. How to study the Bible, stewardship, etc.

Baptism

2

Class Two: Personal Relationship (small groups)

Dealing with personal prayer.

Bible Study and Worship

3

Class Three: Serving Others

Spiritual Gift and Passion Assessments

Missions and Outreach

4

Class Four: Sharing With Others

Understanding and putting into practice.

Teaching and Evangelism

5

Certificate of Completion

Getting plugged into ministry

Fully Functioning Disciple

SHOUT-OUTS

To my family: Quo, Jay, CJ, and Cameron—I love you guys more than you'll ever know. You guys inspire me so much! Mom & Dad, thanks for always believing in me and pushing me to reach beyond what I thought were my limitations. To my church family: Pastor Barnette (you have been the best pastor ever!), Tabitha, and the Peace Baptist Crew, thank you for your endless love and support. The best is yet to come for us! My SYNC Youth Group & Staff, you guys made all of this possible! Thanks for letting me be your youth pastor. What an honor! Maina Mwaura, my big homie, thanks for all the long talks and advice and pranks. You push me to be the best youth pastor I can be. To Anthony Flynn, Milton Campbell, and the Urban Youth Workers Institute family: Thank you for all of your support, love, and free lunches! I'm looking forward to our partnership.

To my GROUP & SYM Family: WOW!!! Thank you guys for this unbelievable opportunity. I'm so humbled. Doug: thanks for letting me wear your name tag all those years. Andy: you introduced me to everyone; without you, none of this would have been possible. Nadim: YOU ARE AMAZING! Bro, I love you to death! Thanks for all your help with this project. Sorry for all of the late e-mails! Veronica: You are an amazing designer! Thank you so much for capturing my heart and vision for this project. I love everything about the layout! Job WELL done! Kami: my soul food eating partner, thank you so much for everything! The next trip is on me. Rick: you have been a great inspiration to me! Thanks so much for all you do!

To anyone and everyone I missed, please know I am so appreciative for all of the love and support you've given me over the years!